Sock Puppet Madness

Sock Puppet Madness

35 colorful characters to make in minutes

Marty Allen

For my Grandmother, Rose Spano Allen, who taught me everything I needed to know about everything ever. I miss you every day, you're with me every day. My Nana.

Published in 2013 by CICO Books
An imprint of Ryland Peters & Small Ltd

20–21 Jockey's Fields   519 Broadway, 5th Floor
London WC1R 4BW   New York, NY 10012

www.cicobooks.com

10 9 8 7 6 5 4 3 2 1

A CIP catalog record for this book is available from the Library of Congress and the British Library.

ISBN: 978 1 908862 67 9

Editor: Mandy Lebentz
Designer: Ashley Western
Illustration: Marty Allen
Cutout photography: Martin Norris
Background photography: iStock.com

For digital editions, visit www.cicobooks.com/apps.php

Visit www.martystuff.com for more information about the author.

Printed in China

Contents

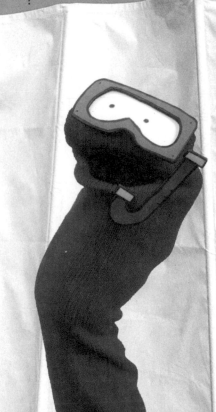

Improper and Inconsequential Introductions

Who Is This Book For

Hi, I'm Marty! I make and sell sock puppets and their portraits. Welcome to my book about how to make your own.

In my brain, this book is for everyone. But let's narrow the scope a bit. First of all, it's for anyone who likes to make things. Also, and not mutually exclusive from this first category, this book is for anyone who is interested in the things that I make. It's probably also for people who like to look at pictures of funny creatures and learn the stories about them.

But the more refined point that I want to make is aimed at those who wish to make the designs that I have laid out. This book is intended for all ages, but in all likelihood the ambition should be modified depending on the age of the maker(s). In all instances, a parent or guardian or crafty friend knows better than I do what sort of activities any given young person can handle (as we are all quite different), so please consider this a loose guideline.

The major issue is the fact that all of my projects, while often simple, are created with the help of a (Sacred) Hot Glue Gun (of Power). Much and more can be done without hot glue, and I'll speak in greater detail about this in the body of the book, but if you want to match the recipe precisely, this is the particular spice (or blender, to follow the tool metaphor) that I call for.

If your child is aged six or older and reasonably dextrous, I believe that he or she can handle hot glue, if supervised. If your child is aged eight or up and reasonably responsible, I believe that she or he can make the projects unsupervised. And if you are 47 and think that making puppets is neat, I believe you can do anything, and that you are awesome.

... And How To Use It

In this book, I give you precise measurements for eyes and noses, and all manner of puppety bits and patterns to cut in all sorts of ways. I've taken quite a lot of time to build and measure and trace and draw all of these useful things. I've even included templates for every project (see pp.120–6).

And I have one piece of advice: don't use them. I sort of mean it. Okay, I made the book, so I'm happy if you want to make your own replica of Uncle Monsterface or Lillith Lollybottom and prance them about, extending their story into new places and ideas. As a matter of fact, it would be neat to see, and many of you will probably make better versions than I did. But my true hope is that this book acts as an inspiration and a springboard—first and foremost for puppet-building, but also for character-building, and indeed for any creative projects in general.

In short, as for all of my favorite instruction books through time, I hope that this book inspires you to make your own unique creations.

And one more thing, I strongly recommend that you read through all the basics before digging in: a lot of my techniques are rather specific to the way that I work. Once you get through "The very basic basics" and "The fancy basics," you're qualified to jump around, but check that stuff out or you're likely to say things like, "This makes no sense," and "This man is clearly a crazy person." Even more so.

An Incomplete History of Puppets and Puppetry

Here's the thing to remember: puppets are magic. Let's get a bit of bad news out of the way: among various important people at various fancy-pants dinner parties, sock puppets are not the most respected form of the puppet arts. I'm sure that many intelligent people before me have thought up a variety of reasons why this was the case, and they were all quite wrong.

My pants are fancy

Fancy

Here's the other thing: the history of puppetry is long and varied, and many more qualified folks than me can and have talked and written about it at length. I'm sure these cool histories can be found in your local library, apothecary, or online, and I encourage you to seek them out.

Why do people think the sock puppet is lowly? For the same reason that I think it is great: almost everybody has socks, and anybody can make one. Quick, go for it, I won't watch. Take off your sock, put it on your hand. Tuck in the toe and talk. In a moment, you will have transformed an inanimate object and imbued it with life and feeling. You made a puppet. Magic.

For our much more fun and interesting purposes, here's *The Real History of Sock Puppets* (please don't tell anyone about it):

Every person and creature ever exists in a land called Sock Puppet City (one of the Seven Layers of Space). You, me, everyone you meet, everyone who ever has been or will be and many more in between. We all find our sock puppet selves in time. When not puppeting about, sock puppets often appear among the Seven Layers of Space in small framed photographs called the "Sock Puppet Portraits," hanging on walls and standing on shelves throughout the reaches of time and space. Countless noteworthy scientists and thinkers, such as Professor Hero, Nikolai Tesla, and the Magician Detective, have large collections of them in their homes to advise them.

I, myself, assist in creating and distributing sock puppets and the Sock Puppet Portraits here on Earth. I am a certified Sock Puppet Engineer, and after completing this book, you will be, too. And that's magic.

PART

1

Holy Cannoli! Everything You Ever Needed to Know Ever

Over time, I've developed a distinct style of puppet-building, and it's my intention to share that with you. Puppet-building techniques vary a lot, and this book does not undertake the bold task of teaching you anything more than how I do it. As with all kinds of training, it is my hope that by learning the way I do stuff, you'll develop your own style and techniques.

Achieving the Sock Puppet Mind (SPM)

The first and most important step in your journey to becoming a certified Sock Puppet Engineer is achieving the elusive Sock Puppet Mind (SPM). Here's the trick: relax and have fun (while you make the greatest work of art of all time). Because this is fun. And fun should be fun. Just be careful with the hot glue and scissors, okay?

The next two things you need in order to achieve the SPM (and indeed to get underway with any and all creative projects) are to give yourself the time and the space to do them. Easy, right? Maybe not always so easy in this topsy-turvy fast-moving world of ours but, I'm telling you, you'll thank me later…

Give yourself some time: whatever age you are, carve out two hours of craft time for yourself. Send me that "thank you" note covered in glitter.

Give yourself some space: set aside a little corner (or entire room or house or orbiting ship) as your art or craft (or music or weaving or pickling) area. Again, this applies to all ages. Get some little bins, and get some stickers to label the little bins. It's enormously gratifying…

This same advice for the Sock Puppet Mind applies as equally to making a garden and writing a novel as it does to making a sock puppet—please interchange at will. It will do wonders for your outlook on life.

"Do your work, then step back. The only path to serenity"
Tao Te Ching

Sock Puppet Tools and Supplies, Incorporated (The Shopping List)

Here is all the stuff you need to bring your sock puppets to life and give them the personalities they are crying out for! This is not rocket science (it's more like brain surgery). You could do it with a sock and a pen, but if you want to push your boundaries, here's what I, a certified senior level sock puppet engineer, suggest. Most of what you'll need to do and all the lessons are given in this book.

Socks!

Clearly, we need socks… (or at least one). And here's the thing: any sock works. It doesn't even have to be clean. Unless otherwise noted, most of the socks I use come from an average sock for a man, with a foot sized 10–12 (because that's me). It just so happens that adult socks fit on most hands, too.

Socks can be found in all of the obvious places:
Fancy stores
Cheapo stores
Backs of drawers
Fronts of closets
Behind the dryer (please be mindful of the Lost Sock Vortex)

Socks can be big and little and knitted and fluffy and fancy and plain and all that comes in between. I encourage you to have a growing collection, so that your inspiration has no limitation. Nearly all the lessons call for at least one very specific color of a sock, and some for a specific type of sock. It's okay if you can't find that sock. Shall I repeat this in a larger font? It's okay if you can't find the specific sock I call for.

The shape and size might be a little different, too. This is also okay. As a matter of fact, it's great, because it's nature's way of making an infinite variety of interesting designs, not unlike people and snowflakes and chowders. Each subtle change spells something unique. Go with your gut and find the sock that you think fits the bill.

HOW TO PUT A SOCK PUPPET ON YOUR HAND

For many, this might be self-explanatory, but experience dictates that it needs a moment of reflection. The most important thing to note is that the HEEL of the sock is the BACK of your sock puppet's head. That way, his or her head naturally juts forward, like a flamingo or a llama…

scissors

I use scissors for everything. Sharp ones work best, but are, you know… sharp. So craft ones are cool for smaller hands, too. Here and there a utility knife might come in handy for greater accuracy, but by and large, scissors are just the thing.

safety note: Safety is safe! Scissors can be dangerous! It goes without saying that we should be careful with scissors! Sharp things can, by design, cut us! No running, no sword fights! Don't make me use any more exclamation points, use your head, and don't hurt yourself or others!

Glue

Again, a real staple of most craft construction is glue, the stuff that sticks stuff together, and I mostly call for the use of hot glue and the gun that distributes it. Cold glue and craft glue can come in handy, too. All are available at any craft store. Hot glue guns are surprisingly cheap. Stock up on sticks.

Craft Fur

I use craft fur a lot. It's swell. It usually comes in 8 x 10 in (20 x 25 cm) sheets as well. Again, you might not be able to find just the right color, and you should have a collection of it…

Cardboard

We need it, mostly for mouths. I recycle cereal and cracker boxes because they are the perfect stiffness.

Craft Foam

I use A LOT of craft foam in my projects. The main reasons that I use it are that it is durable, flexible, and comes in an excellent array of colors. It works for lots of ages because it is easy to cut and shape. Craft foam can be found in most major craft stores in 8 x 10 in (20 x 25 cm) sheets. It can also be found in nifty little baggies with cool pre-cut shapes. As with socks, if you can't match the exact color, that's a-okay and just spells more interesting variations. Also, as with socks, I recommend you keep a lot on-hand for various projects.

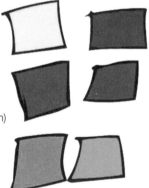

RECYCLING RULES!

Use everything you can find, and get in the habit of collecting things that might come in handy later. Cereal boxes aren't just the right stiffness, but are amazingly colorful, too! A discarded soda tab can make an awesome eyeball! A cast-aside jet engine can make a convincing top hat! Collect whatever inspires you and keep it in your art space. Neatly!

Stuffing, AKA Head Fluff

Most of the puppets I design use a little bit of stuffing pushed up into their heads in order to give them some more shape, definition, and brain power. This, too, can be found at most major craft outlets, or inside of your unfortunate teddy bear or pillow. Do not try to use the kind of stuffing that goes well with turkey, or else your puppet will become delicious.

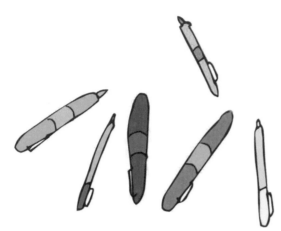

Markers and Pens

A lot of my designs call for you to draw right on the craft foam or puppet to create artistic details—usually pupils. A selection of permanent markers is best, though for the smaller artists, washable markers are acceptable alternatives. Get lots of colors, though black is the one we turn to the most. Which is to say all the time.

Oddments

The lessons call for a lot of little oddments, most of which you can get by without, but, regardless, it's fun to keep a collection of cool stuff that inspires you. An organized collection—I'm not encouraging hoarding! Here and there I ask for the use of buttons, pipe cleaners, ping-pong balls, fluffy pompoms, all that good stuff. Go to the craft store with a little budget in mind and go crazy just building an arsenal of puppety materials. It's a good time.

I encourage you to keep a collection of random stuff that inspires you. You found the perfect piece of foil? A cool, colored paper? Set it aside. That turkey sandwich that Grandma made you in 1994? Maybe you should throw that away.

Needle and Thread (Optional)

Here's an incredibly interesting aside regarding why I don't do much sewing but why you should if you like to sew… (in which case add thread and needle to the tools list). I don't sew because I don't have much of a fondness for doing it. I've tried, I get fussy, stab myself with a needle, and then little heads fall off little bunnies. It's all quite sad. Mind you, the results from a proper sewer are often beautiful, and an enterprising designer could apply almost any of my designs to fabric, at which point I will high-five you 50 times straight. Seriously, sew stuff on if you want to. I like to work with hot glue because it's fast, and craft foam because it's bright, and all of it because I'm impatient. And if you don't like sewing, this book is for you!

The Very Basic Basics

Sometimes you should plan your puppet out meticulously... and other times you should just throw it together and have fun in the moment... and more often than either, you should have a rough idea of what you want but be open to inspiration. Regardless, there are a few techniques that I use throughout the 35 lessons, and I highlight them here in order to lure you in to a sense of false complacency. I hope that, while readying you for the lessons to come, these techniques also ready you for your own creations.

The All-Important Choosing of the sock!

Pick a sock, any sock! Basically, I see the choosing of the sock two ways.
I either let the sock inspire the puppet, or the puppet inspire the sock.

Technique 1: Let the sock inspire the puppet

Perhaps an argyle sock reminds you of a photocopy repairman?

Perhaps a red tube sock brings to mind a water polo champion?

Perhaps that worn out sock is just the fit for a character from "Death of a Salesman?"

Perhaps that simple green sock seems like an incredibly smart and frog-like amphibian who sings songs and stars in TV shows and movies?

Technique 2: Let the puppet inspire the sock

The second technique usually requires a bit more searching and scouring for just the sock you have in mind.

Just the thing for the dentist? An off-white short sock.

The perfect look for the failed artist? A worn-out paint-covered sock.

A perfect space alien? That neon-green knee-high sock.

Sock Puppet Structure, 101

At their most basic, my sock puppets consist of a sock, a cardboard mouth, some head fluff, and some stuff glued to them.

Basic Hot Gluing Techniques (and Final Warnings)

As I mentioned in the introduction (what, you didn't read the introduction?!), all my lessons call for the use of hot glue. Or, as we prefer to refer to it, The (Sacred) Hot Glue Gun (of Power). You are more than welcome to try other types of glue as a substitute. Many will work in many situations. Others might not.

Here's the thing that is neat about hot glue—it works fast, not unlike your child's brain. Working with hot glue, you learn to move quickly and that things will dry quickly and stick together really well, and that's gratifying if you are impatient and small. (It's also gratifying if you are impatient and me.) But here's the less neat thing: if you touch the tip of the (Sacred) Hot Glue Gun (of Power), it burns you, and if you get some glue on you while it's hot, it hurts. It hurts a lot for a second.

So I'll say it once again: be safe with the hot glue. The tip doesn't touch you, nor does the hot glue! If it does, stop immediately and get help with your minor burn. When you are done with the hot glue gun—ALWAYS UNPLUG IT!

Now, having been burned by a hot glue gun A LOT, I think I can safely say that, unless you clutch the hot tip to your eyeball, we're not looking at anything worse than the pain of a scraped knee. And once taught respect of the tool, most people big and small are surprisingly more adept with it. For some of you, this might even mean the end of our trusted friend white glue…

CREATIVITY RULES!

When I give instructions, they are intentionally a little imprecise, leaving what we in the sock puppet business like to refer to as some "wiggle room." This is more like cooking pasta sauce than baking a chocolate cake—add a dash of this and that and substitute liberally—making disaster unlikely. Nothing would make me happier than to see all of these designs remixed into new creations, ideas, and characters, or strange spins on the ones that I've created. If and when you do take it there, or if and when you take it anywhere, share with me and the world. We want to see! I'm giving you lots of guidelines and suggestions, ways to get you fired up and inspired. At the end of the day, it's a sock puppet, and there is no wrong technique (though that blow torch might be ill-advised).

That's my spiel and warning, of sorts. I love hot glue for all manner of projects, and if taught properly to young people, it can really expand horizons, particularly into the third dimension. For work purposes, here is what to remember:

1. It's hot.

2. Move fast because it dries fast.

3. Once it's stuck, it's pretty hard to make adjustments.

Use your hot glue gun with patience and celerity. Celerity is different from celery. The first means quickness, the other means stringy healthy vegetables that taste good with peanut butter. Work toward the first definition.

With all that in mind, I try to have a clear plan before putting any glue in place. I think it through, and often in the case of eyes or specific pieces, I'll put a dot with a marker on the intended target to make sure that my aim is true. Sometimes if it is hard to judge the face of the puppet, I'll position it on a temporary stand (water bottles work well) to make adjustments, or I'll work with the puppet posed on my non-working hand. In some instances I'll call for a lot of glue, in some I'll call for just a dot or so. This depends a lot on the material and the situation.

HOW TO STAND UP CRAFT FOAM PIECES WITH HOT GLUE

My least intuitive use of the hot glue gun is one that I use very often. Most of the lessons with teeth and most of the lessons with parts that "stand," like fins or antennas, call for this technique. Your standard sheet of craft foam has a large flat surface, but it also has a little dimension, making an ⅛ in (3 mm) thick "edge." I use these edges a lot. When gluing objects like teeth so that they "stand up," apply a small strip of hot glue so that it covers the edge, and quickly press the edge to the flat surface and hold for 5–10 seconds. Voilà! Stuff stands up. Reliably, too. It's pretty neat, and the variations are infinite.

Building the Sock Puppet MOUTH

Here it is, subtly tucked away in a sub-chapter, the Super Secret Secret that really separates my sock puppets and yours from the rest of the proverbial pile. The MIGHTY Cardboard Mouth. Understand, this is Serious Business, and I impart this knowledge to you with the implication of your promise. A promise to use this information responsibly.

Repeat after me:

"I (insert name here), do solemnly swear to use The Super Secret Secret of The MIGHTY Cardboard Mouth responsibly, and for the Power of Good. And awesomeness. And Fun."

The oval o' cardboard

A stiff cardboard mouth makes all the difference with your sock puppet friend, and it's as easy as cutting an oval out of cardboard, turning your sock inside out, gluing it in, letting it dry, and then turning it outside-in. Sometimes I call for a sock to end up inside out, in which case you'd start by just gluing the oval to the regular outside of the sock.

Once again, the heel is the BACK of the head. You are gluing the oval on to the exact opposite side. Generally the oval gets hot-glued and firmly pressed down just before the tip of the sock. I encourage you to experiment with this placement and see how it affects various puppets—small changes can yield big differences.

At the beginning of each lesson, I suggest whether the puppet's mouth should be:

SMALL (around 2 x 1½ in/5 x 4 cm—but if it's a teeny-tiny sock, you could even take it down ½ in (13 mm) further with either dimension;

MEDIUM (around 3 x 1¾ in/7.5 x 4.5 cm);

LARGE (around 3¼ x 2 in/8 x 5 cm—again with about ½ in (13 mm) of stretch room upward.

These measurements and the diagrams are a guide, but always take into account the relative size of your sock. The size and shape of your oval will make a big difference as to the character of the puppet, too, so experimentation there is also encouraged.

Though it isn't essential to build your sock puppet with a cardboard mouth, it is highly recommended (and way cooler), as you suddenly go from a floppity sock mouth to a stiff, expressive, and much more convincingly puppeteered mouth. It also acts as a great surface for TEETH! If you do go for it, it should be your first step, as you'll build the rest of your puppet around the mouth and head.

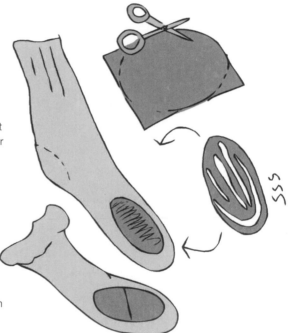

Templates for a small, medium, and large mouth

The oval o' sticky felt

Each time you make a stiff mouth, I also call for you to cut an oval out of sticky felt that is slightly smaller. This oval should be just ⅛–¼ in (3–6 mm) smaller than your main mouth, as it is designed to sit INSIDE the mouth.

Cut out the slightly smaller oval in the designated color. Pull off the sticky backing and set aside, non-sticky side down. As a long-term precaution, also add a small amount of hot glue or craft glue to the interior surface of the mouth. Press the smaller oval firmly down inside the mouth, creating a kind of depth and "inner mouth."

Head Full of stuff

Each of the lessons also calls for the head of the puppet to be stuffed. Again, I either call for a small, medium, or large amount of fluff.

A small amount = a tiny ball that fits between your thumb and forefinger

A medium amount = about twice as much as that

A large amount = just shy of a full handful

As with the mouth, this can be relative. Make a judgment based on both your own sock, and the finished picture of the one provided. Now just stuff that little bit of fluff up into the top of the head. There's no need to glue it in. With some practice and use, your top fingers will slide right beneath the fluff every time.

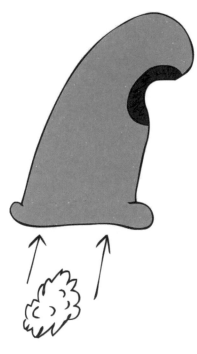

"Edging" and the Almighty Marker of Details

I use markers for a lot of the detailed work, and most commonly to put a pupil in an eye. But one marker technique begs further explanation. I refer to it as "edging." Usually you can get away without these techniques, especially if it's little hands making the project, but it's often what makes the puppet just a little bit nicer.

Perimeter edging

Some lessons call for just the "perimeter" of a piece to be edged. This will commonly be a small shape cut from craft foam. The "edge" once again refers to the ⅛ in (3 mm) thick "edge" of dimension on the craft foam. When I suggest that you "edge" the perimeter, I'm calling for you to darken just the edge.

Perimeter and interior edging

If I call for "interior edging," start by edging the perimeter. Any piece that has interior edging also has perimeter edging. When you create an interior edge, you add extra dimension to the foam piece by continuing the edged line on to the flat surface—typically, just another ⅛ in (3 mm) of interior edging will do.

Using the Puppets, and Puppeteering In General

This seems like a good moment to note a bit more about how this puppet works on your hand.

Your hand slips all the way inside the puppet, making a pointed "C" shape.

Your thumb sticking out forms the bottom jaw.

Your four other fingers sliding beneath the fluff and on top of the cardboard form the top of the head

Experiment with subtle movements and bigger movements. Turn your hand to various degrees, and make the most of the movement of your wrist. When making the puppet "talk," practice moving the mouth up and down with each syllable. It helps to think of the puppet "pushing" the words out of its mouth.

A BRIEF LESSON ABOUT COLOR

Color and design are large parts of the puppets that I build and subjects that could fill whole lifetimes, let alone books. In terms of color, if you feel overwhelmed, you know more than you think. A lot of what I do is created with knowledge of contrasting and complementary colors, but never mind that. If you're looking to experiment, start by simply choosing colors that you think look nice together. Surely you already do this when choosing which shirt to wear? Now look for two different colors that you find in nature and that are appealing to you. Try to replicate those values. Experiment from there.

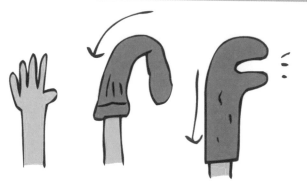

The Fancy Basics

Now let's build some simple sample friends of learning (and justice)! By that I mean a few proper sock puppet characters. From here on out, you'll get not only the "how to," but also a whole personality with each one—I can't help myself! The first creatures were designed to showcase some of the most important features and techniques. As such, I made a few variants of each of these so that you can also see what happens when you change them up. Each section begins with some basic ideas about this particular feature, and then brings you to a lesson applying this knowledge. And without further ado, let's jump into the pool and build a Sock Puppet Army of Friends...

Important note with these instructions: when I refer to left and right, it's referring to the left and right of you looking AT the puppet.

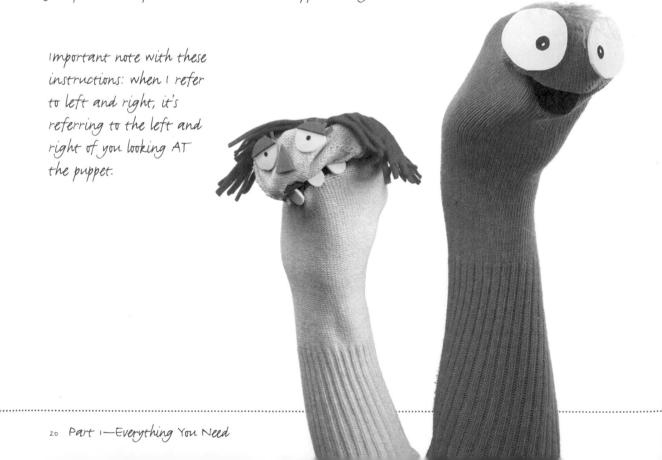

Creating the Sock Puppet EYE(s)

Nine puppet times out of 10, the puppet's eyes are going to be the most important details you add. Whether they are large or small, shifty or straightforward, sleepy-lidded or bugging-out awake, and most importantly where they are placed, will affect your puppet and its personality enormously. The eye is the first place we look to find a genuine emotion.

If you're starting from scratch, it's highly recommended that you work on the eyes once you have the head shape figured out. Eyes can be made from anything. In this book, more often than not, I'll have you cut out a circle, almond, or a rectangle and put a dot in the middle of it and call it an eye. But there are also buttons and ping-pong balls and cloud shapes and more. In short, any shape with a dot in the middle and placed on a face is likely to look like an eye.

Eye placement

It really does matter where you put the eyes. The best way to learn and find out about this is to try it yourself before final gluing, and you will see how the eye placement will drastically shift the mood and personality of your puppet.

For the purpose of this book: I always give you eye coordinates. In every lesson, I base these coordinates on their relative distance above the mouth, and from each other. As with all specifics in this book, we've got the wiggle room, so make your final call based on variables with your own sock and by looking at the picture of the final puppet and, most importantly, by following your heart.

What do I have against goggly eyes? I don't really like them, that's what. Okay, that's an understatement. I hate them. Here's my thing: I feel like they rob the puppet maker, puppet, and puppeteer of the opportunity to add a lot more direction to where the eyes are looking. And that's just so darned important. That said, you can use them and I won't be mad. I get how they are fun and funny, too.

The eyelid

I often call for you to build a little eyelid. I also try to give you a sense of the size—whether it should be half the size of the eye, a little more, or a little less. Sometimes I'll give you a rough measurement. When building the lid, the thing to remember is to initially create the same shape as the eye, but just a hair bigger. Then trim it down to where it needs to be. You never want the white of the eye to extend above the pupil—bad form! And don't be afraid to throw away a misshaped lid and try again. It's always better than gluing the wrong one…

EXTRACURRICULAR ACTIVITY

It was probably Shakespeare, da Vinci, or The Bible (all disreputable sources) who/that said, "The eye is the window to the soul." Take a moment to look at eyes in your favorite works of art and film. From the Mona Lisa to Kermit the Frog, there's a lesson in every one, and a mind that decided where to put them.

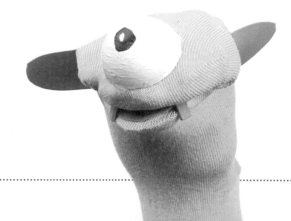

Alberto is a soft-spoken fellow, often found engaging in simple tasks in which he finds great joy, such as organizing objects alphabetically, doing taxes, and eating plain pasta. An avid cyclist and a builder of miniatures, Alberto's favorite things are a warm cup of tea and getting to bed before nine. Also, he can see through walls.

Alberto van Oculon

LESSON 1

This is very exciting... It's our FIRST LESSON TOGETHER! And our first lesson is (the drums are rolling): Alberto van Oculon! Alberto's intended eyes are huge, but to demonstrate how much slight variations affect the overall design, I created two alternate versions of Alberto, one with much smaller eyes in a similar location as the huge ones, and the other with much smaller eyes but placed very differently.

SUPPLIES:

Template on page 120
Orange sock
Cardboard
One square of black sticky felt
One square of white craft foam
Tuft of green boa
Black marker
Head fluff

1 If you want to use templates, copy the one on page 120, then prep the sock utilizing the "cardboard mouth" technique (see pp.17–18). I recommend a MEDIUM oval. Once the sock is reversed, add the oval of black sticky felt for the mouth interior, cut slightly smaller than the cardboard oval, and put a large amount of head fluff in the top for structure.

2 EYES: I'm only explaining Alberto's PROPER eyes. If you like the little ones better, I'm sure you can work it out... From white craft foam, cut out two big 1¾ in (4.5 cm) circles. Using the black marker, add a large ¼ in (6 mm) dot, leaving a little white for the "reflection" in the pupil. Glue directly above the mouth, about ¼ in (6 mm) apart.

3 *HAIR:* Cut out a small tuft of green fur for the hair. Glue it about 1½ in (4 cm) above the mouth, centered.

4 Get ready for a simple evening full of plain food and normal activities. And seeing through walls!

Highly Advanced and Exceptionally Technical Sock Puppet Engineering

Sometimes simple is best. Sure, maybe it's sufficient to leave your new puppet friend streamlined and pure, like so much cool European furniture. But maybe you want to add a ton of other cool crazy things! Here are some ideas, the only limitation being your imagination (and local puppet regulations).

Creating the Sock Puppet TEETH

I'm a big fan of the toothy puppets. Tiny teeth, big teeth, lots of teeth, and a single tooth. They all come to play in these pages. Teeth are almost always created with small squares and rectangles of craft foam, often white but sometimes other colors. The tooth is glued to the mouth, where the "gums" of the puppet would sit—the small gap between the sock puppet oval of sticky felt and the rest of the inner mouth. You utilize the technique described in the section on hot gluing (see p.16), gluing the flat "edge" of the craft foam and holding the piece upward. The intricacies of teeth-making are best exemplified by Uncle Monsterface and Cousin Tinyteeth in Lesson 3 (see p.28).

Creating the Sock Puppet HAIR

Once again, this detail isn't always necessary, but can be fun. I like to play with different hairstyles and techniques—from mohawks to baldness to silly little tufts of hair. Many materials can (and will) be used for hair—yarn, more craft foam, craft poms, even synthetic hairs. But the one I lean on the most is craft fur.

In most cases, craft fur comes pre-glued over a netted base. It has a tendency to push in one direction, like any body of hair, which I'll refer to as the "grain" of the hair. Essentially, some of the fur's length always extends a bit past its netted base. I often use this swooping "grain" to imply a swooping hair-do. This is exemplified by Plim Zambini in Lesson 4 (see p.30).

When gluing craft hair, try to cover as much of the netted surface as possible, paying particular attention to its furthest edges, so that it glues down very flush.

Creating the Sock Puppet NOSE

To nose or not to nose? Who knows? (Ahem. Cough.) The biggest question with noses is whether or not to put one on the face. Sometimes it is just the thing to do; other times it is just a little over the top. Like so much in life, it is a delicate balance.

The tapered triangle
Several techniques are employed throughout this book, but more often than not I'll ask you to create a "tapered triangle." The tapered triangle describes itself. It is more accurately a four-sided quadrilateral, but it "feels" more like a triangle, starting smaller at the top and ending bigger. When appropriate, I provide you with either a diagram or coordinates for the top size and the bottom size. As with everything here, variables are encouraged and expected.

Other shapes and sizes
Any other shape and size that you can imagine can also be a nose, particularly when placed between two eyes. My next most common shape is something circular. But the nose-shaped sky is the limit.

Placement
Placement is also important with the nose, and should generally happen AFTER the eyes and be relative to them.

> ### KEEP YOUR NOSE CLEAN:
> So you made an awesome nose and now you decide you don't want a nose? That's okay. Save it for later! Or better yet, wear it yourself!

Creating Sock Puppet GLASSES

Sock puppet glasses definitely fall under the more advanced techniques. They tend to require some fast moves and delicate gluing of small pieces. They are often based on the notion of a "floating" eye. That is, the eyeball itself is never attached to the head—we only ever see it through the lens. This is best exemplified by Harold Speculex in Lesson 5  (see p.32). In general, the lessons have been ordered by level of relative difficulty, but by way of timely demonstration, Harold is out of order.

Lesson Time

The lessons leading up to this and the three that follow are intended to be a sort of tool kit for making any puppet you can imagine. After this section and throughout the book, lots of other techniques and accessories will be explored and explained (most of which were probably ill-conceived). In these lessons you'll meet beards and moustaches and antennas and bug-eyes and chef hats and robot helmets and all manner of crazy things. Your sock puppet can have or be any of this. Your bespeckled goatee-wearing four-eyed alien with giant ears isn't enough? Your imagination is the limit. What about a peg leg? Vestigial arms? Trendy t-shirts or bags? Bling and piercings? All yours to glue to your sock.

> ### DRAW, AND KEEP A SKETCHBOOK!
> When I first started building a lot of puppets, after I had made dozens and dozens of them, I started to stretch the boundaries of what made sense in terms of a sock puppet creation and style. Or I thought I had... While I actively encourage experimentation, the sock puppet that was essentially a Godzilla action figure glued to a sock crossed a certain deconstructionist line that may have been better left uncrossed. Shortly afterwards, I was hired to create a portrait of a real person in sock puppet form. In carefully studying their face and who they were, I was suddenly moved by how much of a difference a subtle detail or change could make. Artists are always encouraged to draw from life and, unbelievably enough, this was true for me as a sock puppet artist, too. It was more than true, it was transformative. Keep a sketchbook! At this point, the first step in almost every puppet I create is a sketch (unless I'm engaging in pure play). And there isn't a single puppet from this book that I thought up before the Godzilla sock...

Like his nose and that of a famous puppet before him, Wolfgang's name keeps growing. Fortunately it has nothing to do with lying and everything to do with a genetic disorder known as "Wolfgang Nostralia Cucumberbun-Itis." Born W. Umber, as his nose grew, so, too, did his name. From Wolf Cumber, to Wolfgang Cumberbun, to his now-overwhelming title, no one knows if there's room for more. His giant nose gives him the ability to judge a person's character with complete accuracy.

W. N. Cucumberbun

LESSON 2

As with Alberto, I built an alternate version of Wolfgang so that you can see the difference the size and placement of a nose can have on a character.

SUPPLIES:

Templates on page 120
Blue argyle sock
Cardboard
Black sticky felt
Squares of white, yellow, and pink craft foam
Tuft of yellow fur
Black marker
Head fluff

1 If you want to use templates, copy the ones on page 120, then prep the sock utilizing the "cardboard mouth" technique (see pp.17–18). I recommend a MEDIUM oval. Once the sock is reversed, add the oval of black sticky felt for the mouth interior, cut to be slightly smaller than the cardboard oval, and put a medium amount of head fluff in the top for structure.

2 EYES: From white craft foam cut out two ½ in (13 mm) squares. Using your black marker, add two small "shifty" dots, looking right. Glue them ½ in (13 mm) above the mouth and ¾ in (2 cm) apart.

3 HAIR: From yellow fur, cut out a small ½ in (13 mm) tuft. Glue it about 1½ in (4 cm) behind the mouth, centered.

4 NOSE: Wolfgang's true nose is the huge one, but I'm sure you can figure out the littler one if you prefer it. From yellow craft foam, cut out a tapered triangle, about 1¼ in (3 cm) long. The bottom should be about 1 in (2.5 cm), tapering in to about ½ in (13 mm) at the top. Using black marker, edge the perimeter and edge-in. Glue the nose between the eyes with a slight hang over the mouth.

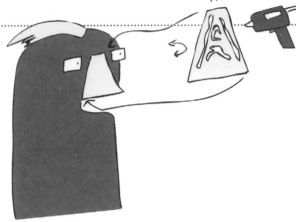

5 TEETH: From white craft foam, cut out three ¼ x ¼ in (6 x 6 mm) squares. Glue them along the top of the mouth, about ¼ in (6 mm) apart.

6 TONGUE: From pink craft foam, cut out a half oval about ¾ in (2 cm) long and ¾ in (2 cm) wide. Cut the flat end at a slight angle. Glue to the folded back of the mouth, so that it pokes slightly out of the right side of the mouth.

7 Go sniff out some trouble, and maybe grow an extra name or two while you're at it…

A BRIEF LESSON ABOUT DESIGN

As with color, design is worth whole careers of study, experimentation, and application. But like color, it is all around you. I apply a variety of principles of design to my work, but again, there is so much that we all know instinctively. One of the most important things when designing is to try some variations. Variations in shape, size, and placement mean everything. This principle sounds simple, but watch what happens if you change the size and placement of the eyeballs in the first lesson, and the size of the nose in the second. That is design. And, as with color, look for examples in the world around you. Design is making choices about how to better communicate your ideas. Everything you see in popular media has been designed, usually quite carefully. Think about why a person made a particular choice when placing a logo or a piece of text in a certain way. Think about why a puppet-maker put an eye in a certain place. Experiment from there…

Uncle Monsterface is, on most days, a misunderstood monster. He is also the leader of the human rock band of the same name. They sing songs about Nintendo and ninjas, and live on Dino Skeleton Island. An excellent dancer and good soul at heart, Uncle Monsterface's intentions are often misunderstood. This probably has a lot to do with his "monster-y" approach to problems. Which is to say he usually bites them or smashes them... But he's a great fellow, and a snazzy dresser to boot.

Uncle Monsterface

LESSON 3 For our final multi-puppet demonstration, you'll see my friendly neighborhood monster, Uncle Monsterface, both with his traditional mouth FULL of yellow teeth, and his bizarre kinsman, Cousin Tinyteeth, for comparison. Uncle Monsterface is the flagship namesake for the human band Uncle Monsterface, often appearing as a gigantic human-sized body-suit puppet on stage as well. The band has released four albums and traveled the country, spreading puppet wonderments!

SUPPLIES:

Templates on page 120
Green sock (inside out)
Cardboard
Blue sticky felt
Squares of yellow, orange, and white craft foam
Black marker

1 If you want to use templates, copy the ones on page 120, then prep the sock utilizing the "cardboard mouth" technique (see pp.17–18). I recommend a MEDIUM oval. Once the sock is reversed, add the oval of blue sticky felt for the mouth interior, cut slightly smaller than the cardboard oval, and put a large amount of head fluff in the top for structure.

2 EYES: Using orange craft foam, cut out two mismatched squares about ¾ x ¾ in (2 x 2 cm) each (but not exactly the same). Glue ⅛ in (3 mm) above the mouth and 1 in (2.5 cm) apart. Using your black marker, add a black dot in the middle of each rectangular eye for a "pupil."

3 *TEETH:* Uncle Monsterface is nothing if not toothy. See the difference between him and Cousin Tinyteeth? Sorry, Cuz, you just don't make the grade! Using yellow craft foam, cut out nine small squares, about ⅛ x ⅛ in (3 x 3 mm), and two rectangles for the front buckteeth, ½ in (13 mm) wide x ¾ in (2 cm) long. Glue slightly irregularly, about ⅛ in (3 mm) apart, making sure the two front buckteeth and the two four teeth go along the top of the mouth, and the remaining five small teeth along the bottom.

4 Dance the night away, Monsterface-style.

THE "FACE" FAMILY OF PUPPETS

Uncle Monsterface is a very special puppet. Any puppet that I build and design with the word "face" attached to the end of its name is automatically one of his LONG LOST KIN. There are several in this book, and the varieties are infinite. All that it takes to add to the "Face" family are three things: rectangular eyes (often but not always orange or yellow), goofy big teeth with gaps, and the desire to make something awesome. Oh, and then add "face" to the end of their name! You've done it! See if you can figure out who else from this book is from the "Face" family, and then help out and add to his never-ending lineage with your own "Face" friend.

Plim is one of the Fabulous Flying Zambinis—a talented trapeze trio. The Zambinis are notorious not only for their prodigious abilities, but also because of the tragic demise of their parents who were accidentally smooshed by an elephant when the kids were small. Plim's sharp mind and good looks are balanced by his crippling social phobias. He hates talking to anyone besides his twin Plom and sister Zimmy, and exits the spotlight as quickly as possible each night under the big top.

Plim Zambini

LESSON 4

Plim is simple and elegant and all about that hair. It's where Justin Bieber stole his 'do! He's noteworthy also because of his unique use of dolls' eyes, an unusual effect that I tend to avoid, but wanted to use to maintain continuity between the whole "family" of Zambinis.

SUPPLIES:

Template on page 120
Pink terrycloth sock
Cardboard
Black sticky felt
Square of white craft foam
Tuft of yellow fur
Small yellow doll's eye
Medium yellow doll's eye
Head fluff

1 If you want to use templates, copy the one on page 120, then prep the sock utilizing the "cardboard mouth" technique (see pp.17–18). I recommend a MEDIUM oval. Once the sock is reversed, add the oval of black sticky felt for the mouth interior, cut to be slightly smaller than the cardboard oval, and put a medium amount of head fluff in the top for structure.

2 EYES: Using scissors or an awl, puncture very small holes ¾ in (2 cm) up from the mouth and 1½ in (4 cm) apart. Push the large eye through the right hole and the small eye through the left hole. Making sure they stay in place, reverse the sock. Add a solid dob of glue to the interior peg of each eye and allow some time for them to dry.

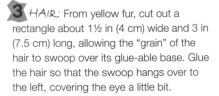

3 *HAIR:* From yellow fur, cut out a rectangle about 1½ in (4 cm) wide and 3 in (7.5 cm) long, allowing the "grain" of the hair to swoop over its glue-able base. Glue the hair so that the swoop hangs over to the left, covering the eye a little bit.

4 *TOOTH:* Using white craft foam, cut out a single small snaggletooth, ¼ in (1 cm) x ½ in (13 mm). Glue it from the right side of the mouth.

5 Get ready for some emotionally complicated circus high dives under the big top…

A WORLD OF STORYTELLING AND FUN ON THE INTERNET

As you may have already started to notice, a big part of the fun of the puppets and their portraits is, for me, telling their story and letting it grow over time. One of the coolest ways I've found is the internet. Many of the puppets in this book appear in videos, on social networking sites, have songs of their own, are in videos for the band Uncle Monsterface, have blogs and all manner of craziness online, and I encourage you to experiment and share in the same manner. The Fabulous Flying Zambinis (Plim, his twin Plom, and their younger sister, Zimmy) star in a rock video set on Coney Island for a song by the band Uncle Monsterface—just one of hundreds of videos. Check it out at youtube.com/unclemonsterface!

Harold is one of the three super Speculex Bros, all so different but with a mutual love of, and dependence upon, glasses. Harold is also an amateur scientist (holding patents in applied flying burrito technologies and experimental aeronautics). His eyeglasses expertise encompasses the complex science of spectacles as well as the science behind eyes and perception. Ladies fall for him like bricks off a bridge, and he's left a trail of broken hearts longer than a line at the post office.

Harold Speculex

LESSON 5

Harold Speculex is the consummate sock puppet with eyeglasses. His techniques apply across a wide array of styles, demonstrating how the eyeball is not always attached right to the head, a notion that isn't obvious...

SUPPLIES:

Templates on page 120
Orange sock
Cardboard
Black sticky felt
Squares of white and blue craft foam
Two small blue craft pompoms
Small piece of paper
Black marker

1 If you want to use templates, copy the ones on page 120, then prep the sock utilizing the "cardboard mouth" technique (see pp. 17–18). I recommend a MEDIUM oval. Once the sock is reversed, add the oval of blue sticky felt for the mouth interior, cut to be slightly smaller than the cardboard oval, and put a large amount of head fluff in the top for structure.

2 EYEGLASSES: From blue craft foam, cut out two 1 in (2.5 cm) circles and "hollow" out ¾ in (2 cm) openings (see pattern). Edge the interior and exterior with a slight "edge in." Cut out two small circles of white paper, sized to fit the hollowed-out openings. Carefully glue each white circle inside the hollowed-out openings. Using a black marker, add a black dot to the center of each eyeball. Using the same blue craft foam, cut out a very small ½ in (13 mm) long glasses bridge and edge the sides and a touch in. Again using blue craft foam, following the pattern, cut out the 2 in (5cm) glasses arms, also edging slightly. Glue the two main eyeholes via the small bridge. Glue the glasses arms so that they point toward the back of the head, applying just a drop of glue and holding in place. Glue the full glasses/eyes so that the bottom of the lenses sit just atop the mouth.

3 *TEETH:* Harold is nothing without his goofy grin. From white craft foam, cut out two ½ in (13 mm) long by ¾ in (2 cm) wide front buckteeth and two slightly smaller teeth. Glue them about ¼ in (1 cm) apart along the top edge of the mouth.

4 *HAIR:* Harold is, like several other sock puppets, proud to be bald. Glue each blue pompom about 1½ in (3 cm) behind the glasses and 1½ in (3 cm) apart.

5 Now get ready to be stunned by Harold's all-too-complete knowledge of your eyeballs. Don't worry, he'll take the edge off by making you the best burrito ever. Don't get too close, ladies!

PART

2

Master Class: Build Your Own Awesome Sock Puppets

Here's the thing... I tricked you, and you now already know how to make any sock puppet you'd ever want to make. All that follows are extensions of those basic techniques. Think of these as some more ideas to get you started. Peppered throughout are some fun new techniques and ideas that might inspire you even more. While I strongly encourage you to make these ideas your own, I fully appreciate that sometimes well-defined boundaries can be just the thing. However they come out, I want to see them! The most important lesson of all has been said before, and I'll say it again: have fun.

Some might call this cool kid from Brooklyn (and guitarist for Werewolf Tuesday) a "hipster." You see, Sebastian really does like all the coolest stuff, from tight jeans to the best bands, but beneath that cool exterior is a great big geek. He loves board games and comics even more than vintage t-shirts and rock shows. He's a great guy to have in your corner, and to style your hair.

sebastian Metaphor

LESSON 6

Sebastian is a very simple puppet, focusing mostly on eye size and placement and the addition of sleepy eyelids. He's like a fancy Plim. This is a pretty specific sock, so feel free to experiment with other socks if you can't find an exact match. There's always another hipster to make! Sebastian Metaphor has a song he wrote himself! Find it on the internet!

SUPPLIES:

Templates on page 120
Striped terrycloth sock
Square of cardboard
Square of blue sticky felt
Squares of white, yellow, and orange craft foam
Small piece of green fur
Black and green markers
Head fluff

1 If you want to use templates, copy the ones on page 120, then prep the sock utilizing the "cardboard mouth" technique (see pp.17–18). I recommend a MEDIUM oval. Once the sock is reversed, add the oval of blue sticky felt, cut slightly smaller than the cardboard oval, and put a medium amount of head fluff in the top for structure.

2 EYES: We'll be doing two large sleepy eyes, with a little extra detail in the pupil. Use white craft foam to cut out two large ovals about ¾ in (2 cm) wide and 1½ in (4 cm) long. In the middle of the oval, make a thick black circle, which will be Sebastian's pupil. Surround the black circle with a thinner green circle, and then outline this circle. Using the eyes you created as a guide, create two identical orange ovals (if just a hair larger). Cut each one in half. Glue these eyelids to the top half of Sebastian's eye. The top of Sebastian's drawn pupil should become obscured, creating a sleepy effect. Yawwwn. Glue eyes just above the mouth about ¾ in (2 cm) apart.

3 NOSE: Using the yellow craft foam, cut out a small tapered triangle about ¾ in (2 cm) long. Glue the nose between the eyes and directly above the mouth. Where noses go!

4 HAIR: Cut out a 2 x 2 in (5 x 5 cm) square from the green fur, being careful to allow for the grain of the fur to hang over the base, giving swoop-style bangs. Glue the hair above the eyes, allowing the swoop to part to the right, slightly over Sebastian's right eye.

5 Take him to the local record store and find some obscure vinyl together. Make sure you ask him about your outfit. He knows what works.

It's true, Puppytron 5000 is from the future; eleven days into the future. According to Puppytron, in eleven days everything is going A-okay. Puppytron's interests include future naps, future sticks, and chasing balls (in the future). He was also recently spotted "dropping beats" as DJ for fellow sock puppet and MC, Auntie Nanaface. It's pretty experimental stuff. Some might even call it futuristic.

Future!

Puppytron 5000

LESSON 7

Puppytron is a very simple puppet, taking great advantage of a lolling tongue and floppy ears. Traditionally, I make Puppytron with a very tiny sock. He's a puppy!

SUPPLIES:

Templates on page 120
Small simple sock (mine actually has little puppies on it, yours doesn't have to...)
Square of cardboard
Square of black sticky felt
Small scrap of brown felt
Squares of brown and red craft foam
Black marker
Head fluff

1 If you want to use templates, copy the ones on page 120, then prep the little sock utilizing the "cardboard mouth" technique (see pp.17–18). I recommend a SMALL oval. Once the sock is reversed, add the oval of black sticky felt, cut slightly smaller than the cardboard oval, and put a very small amount of fluff in the top of the "head" for structure.

2 EYES: Use the black marker to add two black circles for eyes, directly applied to the sock. Each black dot can be about ½ in (1.5 cm) wide, and should sit about ½ in (1.5 cm) above the mouth and ¾ in (2 cm) apart. (While I typically use fancier methods for eyes, I find that a very simple hand-drawn look really suits this little fellow.)

3 NOSE: Using brown felt, cut out a small oval, about ½ in (1.5 cm) wide. Glue the little nose just ¼ in (6 mm) above the mouth, centered between the eyes.

4 EARS: Using brown craft foam, cut out two ovals 3½ in (9 cm) long and 1 in (2.5 cm) wide. Glue the floppy ears on either side of his head. Make sure they are ready for the future.

5 TONGUE: Using red craft foam, cut out a 2 in (5 cm) long oval that is about ½ in (13 mm) wide. At a slight diagonal, snip about ½ in (13 mm) off one side. Glue just the exposed flat edge of the tongue, and press and hold it into the inside crease of the mouth. The tongue should "stick out" and off to the side, silly puppy style.

6 Learn all about life in 11 days with your future puppy friend! Just don't learn too much—time travel has consequences!

One of the stars of the sock puppet soap opera "Sock Puppet Manor," Penelope is the daughter of Gartholomew Durtlinger, and heiress to the Durtlinger Pickle Canning fortune. Aged eight, Penelope was captured by pirates and presumed lost forever. Eight years later, she mysteriously washed ashore with no memory, missing one eye, and having gained an insatiable thirst for power and a love of parrots.

Penelope Durtlinger

LESSON 8

Penelope is another simple puppet, again exploiting the "swoop"-style hair of Plim Zambini (see p.30). Many of her features are very small, so they require some delicate cutting. Also, this is one of the few times I will actively ask you to use a needle and thread, and it's not for structure's sake.

SUPPLIES:

Templates on page 121
Light purple sock
Cardboard
Blue sticky felt
Small piece of black felt
Squares of red, white, magenta, and yellow craft foam
Small patch of yellow craft fur
Fine-tipped black pen or marker
Blue marker
Needle and thread (!)
Head fluff

1 If you want to use templates, copy the ones on page 121, then prep the sock utilizing the "cardboard mouth" technique (see pp.17–18). I recommend a MEDIUM oval. Once the sock is reversed, add the oval of blue sticky felt, cut slightly smaller than the cardboard oval, and put a small amount of fluff in the top of the "head" for structure.

2 EYE: This is a simple, small, lidded eye. The biggest variation is the tiny lashes, keeping our pirate girl properly dainty. Using white craft foam, cut out one small circle, about ¾ in (2 cm) wide. Using the fine-tipped black pen, draw a small circle in the center, leaving a tiny bit of white showing in the middle. Surround that circle with blue, and then outline the blue with one fine line of black to create the completed pupil.

3 Using the yellow craft foam, create the eyelid by cutting out a small circle that is just a hair bigger than the white eyeball, then cutting it in half. Glue the eyelid to the top of the eye, very slightly covering the pupil.

4 EYELASHES: Use the same yellow craft foam and cut out three thin ½ in (13 mm) strips. Don't worry that they are longer than pictured—this will make them easier to work with. Using just a drop of glue, glue them evenly to the top of the lid, fastening them to the top of the white eyeball and beneath the slight lip of the lid. Trim them down until they are just under ¼ in (6 mm). Attach the eye ½ in (13 mm) up and to the left of the mouth, leaving room for the nose and lips.

5 EYEPATCH: A pirate has to have an eyepatch, and Penelope's missing eye is one of the great mysteries of Sock Puppet Manor! Using the piece of black felt, cut out a circle just a bit larger than the eye you already have. Snip off the top eighth, creating an eyepatch shape.

Using the needle and thread, bring about 5 in (13 cm) of thread through just the top of the eyepatch, so that one big stitch is showing. Don't worry about stability—this is cosmetic. Tie the string off so that the patch will rest comfortably atop Penelope's head. Glue only the very top of the eyepatch down so that it can flip up. Feel free to improvise a gruesome eye beneath! The string now acts as a little headband; the only thing firmly attached is the top of the patch.

6 *NOSE:* Using the magenta craft foam, cut out a very small ¼ in (6 mm) tapered triangle nose, and glue just ¼ in (6 mm) above the mouth, making sure to leave room for the top lip.

7 *LIPS:* Using small scraps of red craft foam, cut out two tiny half circles, under ½ in (13 mm) each. Cut a very small indent at the top of either circle, making a tiny "lip" shape. Attach one to the top of the mouth and the other to the bottom, making sure that they will line up when the mouth is closed.

8 *HAIR:* Cut out a rectangle from the yellow fur about 2 in (5 cm) long by 1 in (2.5 cm) wide, being careful to leave some of the fur overhanging to allow for swoop-style bangs. Glue the hair above the eyes, set back to the center of the eyepatch string, allowing the swoop grain to part to the right and go up, slightly over Penelope's right eye.

9 Go and pillage something together. Nicely!

Driven nuts by so often being mistaken for a kitty, the Nutty Bunny was further pushed over the edge due to his many years spent dressed up as a mall Easter Bunny. More recently the Nutty Bunny has embarked upon an ill-fated children's TV show that is also a diet fad that is also a pyramid scheme. He takes mild solace in his eerily robust collection of religious memorabilia. Don't startle him, and don't mention eggs of any kind. Ever.

The Nutty Bunny

LESSON 9

The Nutty Bunny is a simple puppet to create, focused mostly on his big buckteeth, his slightly "too small" bunny ears, and his little whiskers. Handle with care, he's nutty. You can hear a song by the Nutty Bunny online! It's nutty!

SUPPLIES:

Templates on page 121
Pastel terrycloth sock
Cardboard
Green sticky felt
Three squares of white craft foam
Two squares of pink craft foam
One square of yellow craft foam
Head fluff

1 If you want to use templates, copy the ones on page 121, then prep the sock utilizing the "cardboard mouth" technique (see pp. 17–18). I recommend a MEDIUM oval. Once the sock is reversed, add the oval of green felt, cut slightly smaller than the cardboard oval, and put a medium amount of fluff in the top of the "head" for structure.

2 EYES: The Nutty Bunny gets some big, uneven "crazy" eyes that are very easy to construct. Using white craft foam, cut out two 1 in (2.5 cm) circles, making one slightly larger than the other (it's nuttier). Using the black marker, put two black dots in the eyes pointing in odd directions (for the nuttiness). Glue the eyes to the head about 1 in (2.5 cm) above the mouth and ¼ in (6 mm) apart, leaving room for that little bunny nose!

3 NOSE/WHISKERS: Speaking of that little bunny nose… Using pink craft foam, cut out a triangle that is about 1 in (2.5 cm) wide and ½ in (13 mm) tall. Glue, triangle point down, just above the mouth. For the whiskers, using white craft foam, cut out five very thin 2 in (5 cm) strips. Carefully glue each whisker around the lower base of the nose with one dab of glue on the small flat end of the whisker, tucked slightly under the triangular nose. Hold each one in place for 10–20 seconds. These can be a little tricky, so be patient. Glue three on one side and two on the other. It's nuttier.

4 TEETH: Using white craft foam, cut out two 1¼ in (3 cm) long x ¾ in (2 cm) wide rectangles for buckteeth. Glue the flat edge of each to the top of the mouth, leaving a small gap between the teeth.

5 EARS: Using pink craft foam, cut out two ovals, 2½ in (6 cm) long and ¾ in (2 cm) wide. Snip ¼ in (6 mm) off the bottom of the oval, creating a flat bottom for the ear. Cut two complementary ovals in yellow, starting at about 2 in/5 cm and snipping to 1½ in/4 cm, but make each slightly smaller than the pink ovals. These will be the inner ears! Snip the bottoms off these, too. Glue each inner ear to the inside of the larger pink ear, centering it on the bottom and making the bottoms flush. Glue each ear to the head by applying hot glue to the flat bottom of the ear, and then pressing and holding it upright to the top of the head (just like we've been doing with teeth). Hold for 10–20 seconds.

6 Hide some eggs and watch Nutty Bunny freak out. Calm him with carrots and religious mementos.

Some people say that Cousin Wizardface is the most powerful wizard of all time ever. Others say that he just found a really cool hat. But there must be something to it, because he can definitely get a pizza delivered quicker than anyone ever, and who doesn't want somebody with that power around?

Cousin Wizardface

LESSON 10

The funnest thing about Wizardface is making (and decorating) his semi-magical hat. The rest is fairly standard procedure at this point. There's a VERY wizard-y song by Cousin Wizardface out there on the Internet to find...

SUPPLIES:

Templates on page 121
Striped purple terrycloth sock
Cardboard
Blue sticky felt
Squares of pink, blue, yellow, orange, and white craft foam
Black marker
Head fluff

1 If you want to use templates, copy the ones on page 121, then prep the sock utilizing the "cardboard mouth" technique (see pp.17–18) I recommend a MEDIUM oval. Once the sock is reversed, add the oval of blue sticky felt for the mouth interior, cut to be slightly smaller than the cardboard oval, and put a medium amount of head fluff in the top for structure.

2 EYES: Using pink craft foam, cut out two 1 x 1 in (2.5 x 2.5 cm) slightly irregular squares. Using the black marker, add a dot in the center of each. Glue them right above the mouth, about ½ in (13 mm) apart.

3 TEETH: Wizards should floss more often. Using white craft foam, cut out four ½ x ½ in (13 x 13 mm) teeth. Glue each about ½ in (13 mm) apart along the top outer edge of the mouth.

4 *HAT:* It's all about the pointy magic hat, really—everyone should have one. Follow the pattern to build a 5 in (13 cm) cone shape using blue craft foam. Fold it over on itself so that it makes a point, gluing in place along an overlapping seam. Hold for 10–20 seconds for the glue to set.

5 Cut out a yellow star (or other shape) to decorate the front of the hat (I've edged mine). I decorated it further with white paint embellishments and some marker. This might be a good time for sparkles, no? Glue the hat the to the center of the head, adding a circle of glue to the perimeter and quickly pushing firmly to the top center of the head.

6 *EARS:* Using orange craft foam, cut out two half-ovals, each about ¾ in (2 cm) tall. Glue edge down and standing up on either side of the hat, ending about 2½ in (6 cm) apart.

7 Build your own magic hat and order a pizza, and then wait less than 30 seconds for it to come. Tell me that's not magic…

Dr. Alien Eyes's precise abilities as a doctor are hard to pin down. While his bedside manner is legendary, the sound of eight eyes blinking is unsettling, even to the bravest soul. His outer-space origin is likely to be true, since he comes to work in a giant flying saucer. His antenna often hums loudly, mostly disco, making him a hit at parties, and distracting from the gross multi-blinking sound.

Dr. Alien Eyes, M.D

LESSON 11 Dr. A is fun and simple, noteworthy mostly because he has many more eyes than anyone else. His original build—a brown sock with yellow eyes—got lost; this re-build demonstrates that the essence of most of these designs isn't dependent on materials.

SUPPLIES:

Templates on page 120
Yellow sock
Cardboard
Black sticky felt
Squares of orange and pink craft foam
Head fluff

1 If you want to use templates, copy the ones on page 120, then prep the sock utilizing the "cardboard mouth" technique (see pp.17–18). I recommend a SMALL oval. Once the sock is reversed, add the oval of black sticky felt for the mouth interior, cut slightly smaller than the cardboard oval, and put a medium amount of head fluff in the top for structure.

2 EYES: Using orange craft foam, cut out eight mismatched circles, about ¼ in (6mm) each across. Using the black marker, give each circle a dot in the middle for a pupil. Glue the eyes in two uneven rows with very little room between them.

3 *ANTENNA:* Using pink craft foam, cut out the antenna shape from a 2½ x ¾ in (6 x 2 cm) rectangle. Glue it standing up and facing out in the center of his head, about 1 in (2.5 cm) back from the eyes.

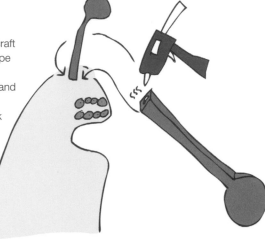

4 Wait for the fever to set in, and when you hear a humming disco beat and your room fills with strange lights, hope that it's Dr. Alien Eyes coming to fix you, and not another hallucination.

The Baron is a proud member of the Old Timey Moustache Society Brigade, three men committed to the greater moustache. A standout among standouts, Claudius sports the "Dali" 'stache. Part-time balloonist, wrestler, and Jungian analyst, his hobbies include collecting striped leotards, fashioning teeth from vanquished foes, taxidermying said foes, and hoarding outrageous lamps. He is known for his incisive psychoanalysis of his fellow so-called "ruffians."

Baron Claudius von Cudgel

The Baron is all about the moustache, and here we have a rare instance of a stiff material being used for hair. The rest is little details, though he also stands out as the one-and-only button-eyed puppet in the bunch. Normally, button eyes feel limited to me in terms of expression but a classic homage to bygone toys felt appropriate here, and this turns out to be one of my favorite designs. Shows what I know...

SUPPLIES:

Templates on page 121
Green and blue striped sock
Cardboard
Green and black sticky felt
Square of magenta felt
Square of yellow craft foam
Tuft of black fur
Mismatched buttons
Head fluff

1 If you want to use templates, copy the ones on page 121, then prep the sock utilizing the "cardboard mouth" technique (see pp.17–18). I recommend a LARGE oval. Once the sock is reversed, add the oval of green sticky felt for the mouth interior, cut slightly smaller than the cardboard oval, and put a large amount of head fluff in the top for structure.

2 EYES: Glue the mismatched buttons about 1 in (2.5 cm) up from the mouth and 1¼ in (3 cm) apart, or if you are ambitious, you can sew them.

3 NOSE: Using yellow craft foam, cut out a 1¼ in (3 cm) long, slightly lopsided tapered triangle, measuring 1¼ in (3 cm) wide at the base. Glue so it sits right above the mouth—be careful to leave plenty unglued at the bottom for the moustache!

4 MOUSTACHE: Using black sticky felt, follow the pattern and cut out two Dali-style swoops. Don't pull the back off, silly! Glue each piece overlapping, tucked under the nose.

5 HAIR: Add a tiny tuft of black fur centered about 1 in (2.5 cm) above the nose.

6 Ready yourself for a hot air balloon-based adventure filled with equal parts hi-jinx and analysis.

Lady McBreath is ambitious, like her shakespearean counterpart, but this would-be queen has her own tragic flaw. she has really bad breath. Not like, lightly offensive breath, as if some off-color salami lurked at the corners of her gums. Her every word is toxic, a withering cloud of wilting disgust. Men weep and entire villages flee as she sings her stinky soliloquies, and she is happy to rule in their absence.

Lady McBreath

LESSON 13

Lady McBreath is a cool and straightforward lady puppet. One of the rare instances of straight-up felt hair, which can be a really fun and effective way to imply long hair.

SUPPLIES:

Templates on page 121
Yellow sock
Cardboard
Black sticky felt
Bright pink felt
Squares of pink, white, purple, blue, and red craft foam
Black marker

1 If you want to use templates, copy the ones on page 121, then prep the sock utilizing the "cardboard mouth" technique (see pp.17–18). I recommend a LARGE oval. Once the sock is reversed, add the oval of black sticky felt for the mouth interior, cut slightly smaller than the cardboard oval, and put a large amount of head fluff in the top for structure.

2 EYES: Cut out two 1 in (2.5 cm) ovals from the white craft foam, and give each a black center dot for a pupil. For each one, cut out ¼ in (6 mm) eyelids from the purple craft foam. Also cut out eight thin ½ in (13 mm) lashes from the blue craft foam. Glue four lashes to the top of each lid. Attach each completed eye ¾ in (2 cm) above the mouth and ½ in (13 mm) apart.

3 NOSE: Cut out a triangle, with each side measuring about ¼ in (6 mm), from the pink craft foam. Glue it centered, about ½ in (13 mm) above the mouth.

4 LIPS: Cut out two lip shapes from the red craft foam, each about ½ in (13 mm) long and ¼ in (6 mm) tall. Add some slight black edging to each. Glue the top lip centered on the top of the mouth, and the bottom lip centered on the bottom. Make sure they match when the mouth is closed.

5 HAIR: Cut out a rectangle, about 6½ x 1¾ in (16.5 x 4.5 cm), from the pink felt. In the middle edges of both long sides of the rectangle, cut a small "divot" (see pattern) to represent indents in the hairline. From either end of the rectangle, cut several 2 in (5 cm) long strips, ¼ in (6 mm) thick, to create hair strands. Repeat with a second piece of felt, but cutting it in half to create two supplemental layers of hair. Glue the first main whole piece to the top of the head. If necessary or desired for "hair body," allow the first piece to dry before adding the other two pieces, layered slightly and maintaining the middle "part."

6 TEETH: Cut out four ½ in (13 mm) half-ovals from the white craft foam. Glue them along the outer rim of the top of the mouth, spaced irregularly, and about ¼ in (6 mm) apart.

7 Grab your facemask and some breath mints.

Born 64.99 million years ago, Spot is really good at hiding. Unfortunately he is also mildly narcoleptic (meaning he falls asleep all the time). He fell asleep hiding behind a rock, and no one found him for 65 million years (or so). He woke up last Tuesday, and quickly became sad that all his friends were extinct. Not one to dwell on his problems, he bought a ukulele, named it "Fossil," and now expresses himself through the therapy of song.

Spot the Elusive Dinosaur

LESSON 14

The most popular Sock Puppet Portrait of all time ever, Spot is loaded with charm. It is unlikely that you'll find the perfect sock to match, but you can certainly capture the spirit of Spot with a few spikes and some darting eyes, and maybe you'll have made a new friend for this lonesome soul. A noteworthy puppet because he is a dinosaur! And who doesn't love dinosaurs?! Spot has real songs you can listen to on the internet! Go find him!

SUPPLIES:

Templates on page 122
Blue terrycloth sock with yellow spots
Cardboard
Blue sticky felt
Squares of white and orange craft foam
Black and yellow markers
Head fluff

1 If you want to use templates, copy the ones on page 122, then prep the sock utilizing the "cardboard mouth" technique (see pp.17–18). I recommend a MEDIUM oval. Once the sock is reversed, add the oval of blue sticky felt for the mouth interior, cut slightly smaller than the cardboard oval, and put a large amount of head fluff in the top for structure.

2 EYES: Using white craft foam, cut out two 1 in (2.5 cm) circles. Using a black marker, add a small black dot to each circle, making each one slightly off-center, "looking" right. Glue each eye about ¼ in (6 mm) up from the mouth and ½ in (13 mm) apart.

3 TEETH: For some odd reason, I color Spot's teeth rather than using actual yellow foam. I'm not sure why, but I don't mess with his perfection... Using white craft foam, cut out five triangles, ½ in (13 mm) long and ¼ in (6 mm) wide at the base. Using a yellow marker, color the front of each tooth yellow. Glue the teeth to the top rim of the mouth, yellow-side out, about ¼ in (6 mm) apart.

4 SPIKES: From the orange craft foam, cut out four triangles 1–1½ in (2.5–4 cm) tall and 1–1½ in (2.5–4 cm) wide at the base, looking to make a slight variety of small to big. Edge just the perimeter of each with a black marker. Glue them, standing up, to the top of his head in the middle, one behind the other. Hold each in place for 10–20 seconds while gluing.

5 Grab a wash-tub bass and an old jug and start up your very own old-timey dinosaur band.

semi-retired member of the Interspatial Explorers' Society, Auntie Nanaface acts as a grandmother to all sock puppets, and to you if you'd like, too. When she isn't cooking pasta or adventuring, Nanaface dabbles in artistic pursuits—most passionately in watercolors and hip-hop. She drops rhymes about manners, a technique learned on a jaunt to Planet Hymnalia, World of Song. She's accompanied by DJ Puppytron 5000. They wear jumpsuits and are pretty fly.

Auntie Nanaface

LESSON 15

Nanaface is something of an homage to my own wonderful grandmother. The most notable detail is her hair, which is a fun experiment mixing fibers, and might be tricky to replicate. The sock pictured is an unusual and pretty pricey find, and I'm sure Nanaface would work just as well with a light gray sock. Listen to her hip-hop song about manners online!

SUPPLIES:

Templates on page 122
Gray mohair sock
Cardboard
Black sticky felt
Squares of yellow, pink, blue and a scrap of red craft foam
Gray and blue yarn
Purple marker
Head fluff

1 If you want to use templates, copy the ones on page 122, then prep the sock utilizing the "cardboard mouth" technique (see pp.17–18). I recommend a MEDIUM oval. Once the sock is reversed, add the oval of black felt, cut slightly smaller than the cardboard oval, and put a small amount of head fluff in the top of the head for structure.

2 EYES: Using pink craft foam, cut out two slightly irregular ¾ in (2 cm) squares, one a little larger than the other. Using a purple marker, add a dot in the middle of each for a pupil. Glue just ¼ in (6 mm) above the mouth, the larger eye on the left, leaving only about ¼ in (6 mm) between each eye.

3 GLASSES: Using blue craft foam, cut out two 1½ in (4 cm) half circles. Carefully cut a ¾ in (2 cm) opening in each one to create the glasses frame (see pattern). Unlike with previous glasses and eyewear, these are going to appear a little more loosely on the face, as if perched on Nanaface's nose, and the eyeballs will not be directly attached to the lens.

Using a scrap of red craft foam, cut out a very small ⅛ in (3 mm) straight bridge for the glasses. Now glue the two eye-frame pieces together with the little red bridge. Glue the finished glasses directly onto the eyes, but perched a little low (see picture), so that it looks like she's peering over them.

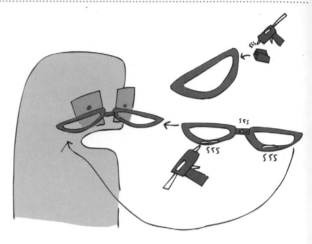

4 TEETH: Using yellow craft foam, cut out six small rectangles each about ⅜ in (9 mm) by ½ in (13 mm), with some irregularity encouraged. Glue each tooth, applying glue to the top edge and holding to the underside of the mouth. Begin toward the back of the mouth, leaving a little ¼ in (6 mm) space between each tooth and traveling to the other side, gluing each in place.

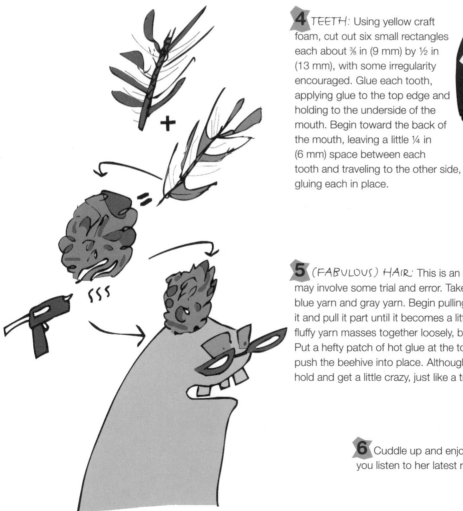

5 (FABULOUS) HAIR: This is an experimental technique, and may involve some trial and error. Take about 4 in (10 cm) of both blue yarn and gray yarn. Begin pulling the yarn at its fibers. Tease it and pull it part until it becomes a little "fluffy." Now mix the two fluffy yarn masses together loosely, building a "beehive" structure. Put a hefty patch of hot glue at the top of Nanaface's head, and push the beehive into place. Although her hairdo is loose, it will hold and get a little crazy, just like a true granny.

6 Cuddle up and enjoy her famous meatballs while you listen to her latest rhymes about manners.

"Sock Puppet Manor" star Phineas is an elephant and a thug. A gentleman at heart, Phineas's commitment to his craft (of "thuggery") is matched only by his cloying need for a friend. A connoisseur of baths, oysters, and couches, Phineas is the thinking man's hit man (unlike his cohort Tony Imhotep—see p.91). Off-screen, Phineas is an elephant named Stompy. He was captured by poachers and performs under duress and constant supervision.

Phineas von Cliven III

LESSON 16

Phineas is a pretty neat construction, a much more complicated version of what we try with Professor Hero (see p.64), pushing the sock boundaries with some creative use of folded felt. He definitely takes a little experimentation, though, as a lot of the pieces are sort of "built to fit." You may need to make adjustments to the patterns based on the sock you find.

SUPPLIES:

Templates on page 122
Light blue or gray sock
Cardboard
Black sticky felt
Squares of white, purple, and red craft foam
Square of gray or blue felt (try to match sock)
Pipe cleaner
Black marker
Head fluff

1 If you want to use templates, copy the ones on page 122, then prep the sock utilizing the "cardboard mouth" technique (see pp.17–18). I recommend a MEDIUM oval. Once the sock is reversed, add the oval of black sticky felt for the mouth interior, cut slightly smaller than the cardboard oval, and put a medium amount of head fluff in the top for structure.

2 TRUNK: Phineas is all about the nose! Using the gray or blue felt, cut out an oblong strip about 6 in (15 cm) long and 2½ in (6 cm) wide) in the shape of the nose (see pattern). Lay the pipe cleaner in the middle. Fold the tapered side of the felt on itself, and tuck over about ½ in (13 mm). Glue along the seam, leaving the circular side "open." Use the black marker to add the nose "rib" details.

3 EARS: Using the same blue or gray felt, cut out identical gray ovals about 2½ x 2 in (6 x 5 cm). Fold and pucker at the bottom, and glue standing up on either side of the head.

4 EYES: Phineas's eyes are a bit unusual in that they stand up on the head, like many spikes or ears from past lessons. Using white craft foam, cut out two 1 in (2.5 cm) squares. With your marker, give each a large black pupil dot. Using purple craft foam, cut out two ¾ in (2 cm) squares for the eyelids. Glue each one "standing up," set back about ¾ in (2 cm) from the mouth, and ½ in (13 mm) apart.

5 BOW TIE: Phineas keeps it classy with his little red bow tie. Using red craft foam, cut out a small ½ in (13 mm) circle. Using the unstoppable black marker, edge around the perimeter and edge in. Using more red craft foam, cut out two uneven tapered triangles (see pattern). Using the black marker, edge the perimeter of each triangle and edge in. Glue the pieces together in the shape of a bow tie. Glue the "knot" of the tie 1 in (2.5 cm) below the mouth.

6 Get ready for an unsettling and one-sided conversation about oysters and baths. Don't remove his chains.

Pete is weapons expert for elite superhero team, The Lava Men, ancient protectors of Dino-Skeleton island. When not being an elite protector, Pete enjoys playing video games and gardening in his enormous hedge maze that he often gets lost in. Pete is a master with his katana and ninja stars, but some of the more subtle ninja arts elude him. The whole "sneakiness" thing falls apart, mostly because he moves too slowly and likes to eat crunchy snacks all the time.

Pete the Notable Ninja

LESSON 17

Pete the Ninja boasts the odd accomplishment of being the sole puppet made of TWO socks. Other than that, he's pretty easy, if a bit finicky to puppeteer. He's the first of the three "Lava Men" in the book—a large superhero team of archetypal characters, featured in Uncle Monsterface's album "Rise of the Lava Men."

SUPPLIES:

Templates on page 122
Dark blue sock
White sock
Cardboard
Black sticky felt
Squares of white and blue craft foam
Black marker
Head fluff

1 If you want to use templates, copy the ones on page 122, then prep the WHITE sock utilizing the "cardboard mouth" technique (see pp.17–18). I recommend a MEDIUM-sized oval. Only add the interior cardboard mouth, we will add the oval of sticky felt later! Add a lot of head fluff.

2 NINJA BODY: We're going to cover one sock with another in order to create the ninja body suit! So, with the white sock already puppeteered on your hand, pull the dark sock over.

3 EYE SLIT: Cut a slit where the eyes will fall, about 2 in (5 cm) wide just above the mouth. Push the fabric in over the mouth without over-stretching and glue in the oval of black sticky felt, so that the mouth oval is over the exterior sock. Add a strip of glue along the circumference of the eyeholes to keep the "under-sock" from slipping out of place.

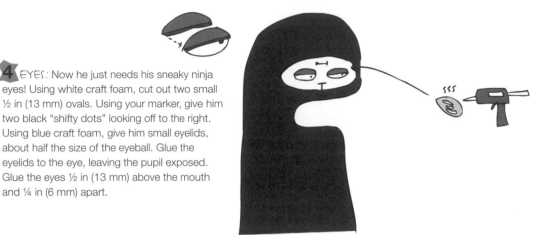

4 EYES: Now he just needs his sneaky ninja eyes! Using white craft foam, cut out two small ½ in (13 mm) ovals. Using your marker, give him two black "shifty dots" looking off to the right. Using blue craft foam, give him small eyelids, about half the size of the eyeball. Glue the eyelids to the eye, leaving the pupil exposed. Glue the eyes ½ in (13 mm) above the mouth and ¼ in (6 mm) apart.

5 Fire up the Playstation and get ready to be pummeled, though be aware that you'll suffer from a nagging frustration that this super-cool, shape-shifting martial arts expert is kind of squandering his time.

Professor Hero is famed for his pioneering inventions, including the Glomtrulious Device, Old Timey Automatons (OTAs), and his shnozel Flixim, a nose tube that acts as a bridge between the various layers of space. And looks like his big nose. A life dedicated to invention has left him almost incapable of communicating with others. Some argue that this was why he created the OTAs, the malfunctioning robots he keeps in his lab. Perhaps he built them as friends?

Professor Hero

LESSON 18

The good Professor is a real oddball straight from my imagination. He's an example of transforming a quirky doodle into a reality. He ends up quite simple, with an easy-to-create nose tube (or "shnozel Flixim") and elegant little eyes. He's one of several characters in "Theodore and The Seven Layers of Space," a trilogy telling the story of the sock puppets, their portraits, and much more.

SUPPLIES:

Templates on page 122
Yellow-toed sock (inside out)
Cardboard
Black sticky felt
Small square of blue felt
Two small beads
Head fluff

1 If you want to use templates, copy the one on page 122, then prep the sock utilizing the "cardboard mouth" technique (see pp.17–18). I recommend a SMALL oval. Once the sock is reversed, add the oval of black sticky felt for the mouth interior, cut slightly smaller than the cardboard oval, and put a medium amount of head fluff in the top for structure.

2 EYES: Glue the two small black beads 1¼ in (3 cm) above the mouth and 1¾ in (4.5 cm) apart, almost on opposite sides of his head.

3 SHNOZEL FLIXIM (NOSE): Using blue felt, cut out a rectangle about 5 in (13 cm) wide and 3 in (7.5 cm) long. Fold it in on itself to create a tube, so that the opening will cover all of Prof Hero's "face," leaving a hole of about 1½ in (4 cm). Glue along the overlapping seam to form the tube. Place the tube above the top of his mouth and glue along its circumference. Hold in place.

4 Now create some confusing inventions together, relishing the awkward silences.

The Earclops is a cyclops with two big old ears. A regular fellow who happens to be a green monster with a giant eye, the Earclops likes rollerblading and completing challenging crossword puzzles, often shouting, "Take no prisoners!" and "This is my destiny!" while finishing the last intimidating multi-syllabic clue of the latest daily in pen. Sadly his greatest dream is to watch a 3D movie, a dream that will never come true due to the whole one-eyed thing.

The Earclops

LESSON 19

The Earclops is a fun little fellow, notable as the one-and-only single-eyed entity in the mix. I thought it wise to make his eye really stand out—by utilizing the classic ping-pong eyeball! Ping-pong eyeballs can and should be used all the time; they are super fun and expressive. Try gluing two together, adding pupils, and putting them on ANYTHING. Sudden (and hilarious) life will be instilled into your bag, fridge, toilet, park bench, etc.

SUPPLIES:

Templates on page 122
Bright green sock
Cardboard
Brown sticky felt
Squares of pink and orange craft foam
Ping-pong ball
Black marker
White paint
Head fluff

1 If you want to use templates, copy the ones on page 122, then prep the sock utilizing the "cardboard mouth" technique (see pp.17–18). I recommend a MEDIUM oval. Once the sock is reversed, add the oval of brown sticky felt for the mouth interior, cut slightly smaller than the cardboard oval, and put a large amount of head fluff in the top for structure.

2 EYES: Get a ping-pong ball (available at all reputable sporting goods stores and aisles). There's no time to play with it! Cut the ping-pong ball in half! It can be a bit tricky to get an even cut—poke scissors through and slice around. A supervised straight razor might make it easier. Essentially, we're looking for an even bottom. While it's already white, I like to paint the ping-pong ball with a coat of flat white just to really make it pop. Then add a black eyeball with your old friend, the black marker.

Glue the half-ping-pong to the sock, ½ in (13 mm) above the mouth. Glue all the way around the exposed circumference and press down quickly.

3 *EARS:* Using pink craft foam, cut out two ear shapes, each about 1½ in (4 cm) long and 1 in (2.5 cm) wide, though some un-even-ness is recommended. Glue them, set back, about ½ in (13 mm) from the mouth on the sides of his head.

4 *TEETH:* Using orange craft foam, cut out two rectangular fangs, about ¼ in (6 mm) wide and ½ in (13 mm) long. Glue them 1 in (2.5 cm) apart along the top of the mouth, wide buckteeth style. Don't try to chew anything complicated.

5 Now get ready for a day at the movies filled with crosswords and roller-blading fun. Just no "Avatar" 3D.

Sock puppet Abraham Lincoln is similar in most ways to his human counterpart. He was the 16th Sock Puppet President of the Sock Puppet USA, serving from March 4, 1861 until his assassination. A noteworthy difference is that sock puppets are invincible unless completely destroyed, so he recovered nicely and moved to a llama farm. Unlike his human counterpart, he is also super good at making paper planes and throwing huge theme parties.

Abraham Lincoln

LESSON 20 Yay! It's our first "real" person puppet! Abraham Lincoln is a pretty simple puppet, though we see a big hat for the first time. As I've mentioned, when you meet "real" people among these puppets, note that they are the sock puppet versions of their human counterparts. There are subtle differences. Abraham Lincoln is one of the first famous people I made as a puppet; his design is simple and he holds a special place in my heart.

SUPPLIES:

Templates on page 123
Gray sock
Cardboard
Green sticky felt
Squares of yellow, white, and black craft foam
Gray fur
Black marker
Head fluff

1 If you want to use templates, copy the ones on page 123, then prep the sock utilizing the "cardboard mouth" technique (see pp.17–18). I recommend a LARGE oval. Once the sock is reversed, add the oval of green sticky felt for the mouth interior, cut slightly smaller than the cardboard oval, and put a medium amount of head fluff in the top for structure.

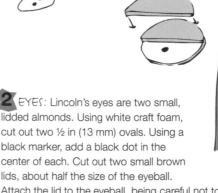

2 EYES: Lincoln's eyes are two small, lidded almonds. Using white craft foam, cut out two ½ in (13 mm) ovals. Using a black marker, add a black dot in the center of each. Cut out two small brown lids, about half the size of the eyeball. Attach the lid to the eyeball, being careful not to cover over the eye dot—nobody wants a sleepy president. Glue each eye ⅛ in (3 mm) up from the mouth, and ¼ in (6 mm) apart.

3 NOSE: Mr. Lincoln commanded the respect of the nation, and he had a big old nose! Using yellow craft foam, cut out a 1 in (2.5 cm) long tapered triangle, ½ in (13 mm) wide at the base. Glue it tucked tightly between the eyes, slightly overhanging the edge of the mouth.

4 BEARD: Cut out a rectangle of gray fur about 3 in (7.5 cm) long x 2 in (5 cm) wide. Glue along the edge of the bottom of the mouth, letting the remainder hang forward over his body.

5 HAIR: Using more gray fur, cut out a small rectangle about 1½ in (4 cm) x 1 in (2.5 cm). Glue it about 1½ in (4 cm) back from the eyes, slightly to the left, in order to leave room for his mighty hat.

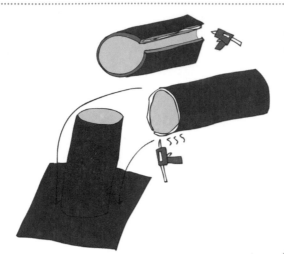

6 MIGHTY HAT: Is it the hat that makes the man or the man that makes the hat? Here, the two details are nearly inseparable, and no Lincoln is complete without his stove-top hat. It's what makes him so Lincoln-y! Using black craft foam, cut out one 2½ x 3 in (6 x 7.5 cm) rectangle for the base and one 2½ x 5 in (6 x 12.5 cm) rectangle for the stove-pipe. Roll the stove-pipe piece in on itself to form a cylinder, and glue along its overlapping seam to keep it together. Now glue that to the center of the hat base, applying glue along its open circumference.

7 Using another scrap of black craft foam, add a circle to size at the top of the hat (unless you'd like something comical to pop out)—the opening should be about 1½ in (4 cm).

8 Glue the hat to the top of the head, perching slightly to the right so that the hair is showing. And now enjoy a rousing paper airplane-building lesson while prepping for a toga party with one of history's great sock puppet luminaries.

An ornery bar-keep from the City of Boston, Bawston the Cat enjoys the Red Sox and eating most of his meals at Dunkin Donuts. Bawston resents the fact that he is only capable of going to the bathroom in a big pile of sand, and he plays a mean harmonica (when persuaded). Don't sass him or ask for one of his famous magic tricks. If he does it, he does it. You'll spoil it and sour his already questionable temper. Plus, he bites.

Bawston the Cat

LESSON 21

Bawston is a nice and simple kitty puppet, with the possibility of infinite variations. For me, he's a salute to my roots (being from Boston myself), so I accentuate the fact that he, like so many of my Boston contemporaries, is rough around the edges. He's got a song online, too! It's ornery!

SUPPLIES:

Templates on page 122
Light red sock (inside out)
Cardboard
square of black sticky felt
squares of white, red, and pink craft foam
Black marker
Head fluff

1 If you want to use templates, copy the ones on page 122, then prep the sock utilizing the "cardboard mouth" technique (see pp.17–18). For this sock, prep the cardboard mouth before turning the sock inside out. (We want the inside out "rag-tag" look to show on the final puppet, so you may need to snip some stray strings at your discretion.) I recommend a MEDIUM cardboard oval. Once the sock is reversed, add the oval of black sticky felt, cut slightly smaller than the cardboard oval, and put a small amount of head fluff in the top for structure. And brains.

2 EYES: Bawston uses the simple lidded eyes technique. Using white craft foam, cut out two small ¾ in (2 cm) ovals. Using the marker, add a small black oval in the lower center of the oval. Using the red craft foam, cut out two circles slightly larger than each eye. Cut each one in half, and then glue onto the white craft foam to create an eyelid. Glue the eyes to the head about 1 in (2.5 cm) above the mouth and 1¼ in (3 cm) apart, leaving sufficient room for the nose and whiskers.

3 NOSE: Using the red craft foam, cut out a ¾ in (2 cm) wide oval for the nose. Glue it on centered between the eyes, just above the mouth.

4 WHISKERS: Using white craft foam, cut out five thin strips 1½ in (4 cm) long—some irregularity is encouraged here. Attach them individually, applying a little glue to the tip and then holding the whisker just beneath the edge for 10–20 seconds. Be patient: whiskers can be frustrating.

5 TOOTH: Using white craft foam, cut out a triangle measuring ½ in (13 mm) on each side, to act as the snaggletooth. Glue the flat edge to the top underside of the mouth, on the right side.

6 EARS: Using pink craft foam, cut out two slightly irregular triangles, measuring about 1 in (2.5 cm) on each side. Take a small chunk out of one of them (he lost it in a fight). Glue the triangles to the head, setting them about 1 in (2.5 cm) behind the eyes, standing up. They should land about 1 in (2.5 cm) apart.

7 Head out to an alley, get into a tussle, and then talk about the Sox.

Chef Bearface was formerly a boy who dressed as a bear. Or a bear dressed as a boy dressed as a bear. No one's sure anymore. At any rate, he decided to follow his dream of becoming a chef. His use of peanut butter cups in everything from cakes and pies to salads and soufflés has earned him a reputation for culinary innovation. He's also a champion napper, dozing off dozens of times a day in unlikely places—often (scarily) inside ovens and casseroles.

Chef Bearface

LESSON 22

Bearface is a simple design, making nice use of a 2D hat and some sly eyes, combining my love of the "monsterface-style" characters, chefs, and bears!

SUPPLIES:

Templates on page 123
Brown sock
Cardboard
Black sticky felt
Squares of white, yellow, and magenta craft foam
Black marker
Head fluff

1 If you want to use templates, copy the ones on page 123, then prep the sock utilizing the "cardboard mouth" technique (see pp.17–18), starting with the sock right side in so it ends reversed. I recommend a MEDIUM oval. Once the sock is reversed, add the oval of black sticky felt for the mouth interior, cut slightly smaller than the cardboard oval, and put a medium amount of head fluff in the top for structure.

2 EYES: Using yellow craft foam, cut out two rectangles ¾ in (2 cm) long by ½ in (13 mm) wide (slightly uneven). Using black marker, add dots just right of center for a somewhat "sneaky" look. Glue the eyes ¼ in (6 mm) above the mouth and ½ in (13 mm) apart.

3 TEETH: Using white craft foam, cut out two squares, about ½ x ½ in (13 x 13 mm), for the front buckteeth, and two smaller squares, about ¼ x ¼ in (6 x 6 mm) for the back teeth. Glue them to the top of the mouth, about ¼ in (6 mm) apart.

4 *HAT:* And now for the all-important chef's hat! Using white craft foam, cut out a rectangle about 1½ in (4 cm) long and 1 in (2.5 cm) wide. Cut out a ½ in (13 mm) tall cloud—a long half circle with three indents and one straight side that is 1½ in (4 cm) wide (see hat-top pattern). Glue the two pieces together so that the hat top sits on top of the white rectangle. Glue the completed hat standing up about 1 in (2.5 cm) behind the right eye, skewed to the right of the head and facing outward, as pictured.

5 *EARS:* Using magenta craft foam, cut out two half-circles, about ½ in (13 mm) tall and ¾ in (2 cm) wide. Glue the left ear 1 in (2.5 cm) behind the left eye, in line (along the same plane) with the hat. Judge the right ear based on the hat, putting it ¼ in (6 mm) away from the hat, on the outside of the head.

6 Get ready for the best peanut butter cup ratatouille this side of the Mississippi, followed by a championship power nap.

Earth science professor and semi-professional whistler, Herb's dream of pro-whistling never quite took off. Left a little sad, Herb fused his seemingly disparate interests into a career as a writer of sci-fi stories. His "Fantastic Tales of the Hollow Earth" series has been published in periodicals, such as "Weird & Weirder Happenings Monthly," while his story "Whistling Harold and the Giant Mole" won an award for Best Existential, Topological, or Nautical short story.

Herb Bloomquist

LESSON 23

This is a motif that I visit a lot and we've already seen as Harold Speculex (see p.32), the balding and awkward nerd. Don't tell Harold, but Herb is probably my favorite ever. There's something so desperately sweet about him... and he's got a song online!

SUPPLIES:

Templates on page 123
Blue terrycloth sock
Cardboard
Blue sticky felt
Squares of yellow, white, red, and black craft foam
Brown yarn
Blue marker
Head fluff

1 If you want to use templates, copy the ones on page 123, then prep the sock utilizing the "cardboard mouth" technique (see pp.17–18). I recommend a LARGE oval. Once the sock is reversed, add the oval of blue sticky felt for the mouth interior, cut slightly smaller than the cardboard oval, and put a large amount of head fluff in the top for structure.

2 EYES: Using black craft foam, cut out two small black ⅛ in (3 mm) dots. (The black beads from Professor Hero, p.64, would be an excellent solution here, too.) Glue 1 in (2.5 cm) above the mouth and ¾ in (2 cm) apart.

3 NOSE: Using red craft foam, cut out a 1 in (2.5 cm) long tapered triangle, measuring ½ in (13 mm) wide at the base and tapering to ¼ in (6 mm). Glue the nose just above the mouth, centered between the eyes.

4 TEETH: Using white craft foam, cut out eight slightly irregular ⅛ x ⅛ in (3 x 3 mm) squares. Glue them irregularly along the top of the mouth, about ¼ in (6 mm) apart.

5 HAIR: Take two sections of brown yarn, about 4 in (10 cm) long. Ball up each section and pull at it to distress it and give a frizzy look. Glue each section on either side of the head, about 1 in (2.5 cm) above the mouth and 3 in (7.5 cm) apart. Add a small tuft of thinned-out yarn across the middle of the head, connecting the two balled-up sections to create the sense of a bad "comb-over."

6 *TIE:* Using yellow craft foam, cut out a ½ in (13 mm) circle to create the "knot." Also from the yellow foam, cut out the 2½ in (6 cm) pointed strip for the actual tie. Glue the two pieces together to create the "tie" shape. Using thin blue marker or pen, lightly stripe the tie diagonally. Glue it to his center chest (where ties go…) about ½ in (13 mm) below his mouth.

7 *SHIRT:* Using white craft foam, follow the "collar pattern" and cut out a collar 2½ in (6 cm) long x ¾ in (2 cm) wide, cut diagonally at both ends.

8 Pucker up and get ready to whistle. For science!

Sgt. B is a tough-as-nails punk rocker with a softer side. As often as you'll find him in a scuffle at the local watering hole, you'll also find him sneaking out to the local animal shelter. You see, Sgt. B has an apartment full of strays. Just don't mention it, unless you want a broken nose. Better to bring up the works of JRR Tolkien. Favorably. Hopefully you share his love of Middle Earth, though, or you'll be due for yet another scuffle.

sgt. Bullocks

LESSON 24

Sgt. B might be a bit tough to find a matching sock for, but as ever, rough approximations are always acceptable. Noteworthy not just because of his punk rock awesomeness, but because of the use of real hair gel to keep his mohawk aloft, Bullocks is a personal favorite of mine. Check out his punk rock song online!

SUPPLIES:

Templates on page 123
Awesome rainbow sock
Cardboard
Green sticky felt
Squares of white, light green, yellow, and red craft foam
Strip of green fur
Small safety pin
Head fluff
Hair gel

1 If you want to use templates, copy the ones on page 123, then prep the sock utilizing the "cardboard mouth" technique (see pp.17–18). I recommend a LARGE oval. Once the sock is reversed, add the oval of green sticky felt for the mouth interior, cut to be slightly smaller than the cardboard oval, and put a medium amount of head fluff in the top for structure.

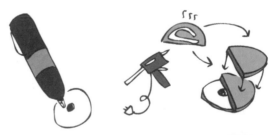

2 EYES: Sgt. B looks a little sleepy all the time, but don't let him fool you… Using white craft foam, cut out two ¾ in (2 cm) circles. Add large centered dots for pupils with a black marker. Using green craft foam, cut out eyelids for covering half the exposed eye. Glue lids to eyes, covering half the pupil for a "sleepy" look. Glue the eyes ¼ in (6 mm) above the mouth and 1¼ in (3 cm) apart.

3 NOSE: Using green craft foam, cut out a tapered triangle, about ¾ in (2 cm) long with a ¼ in (6 mm) top and slightly wider bottom. Puncture the bottom right of the nose with a safety pin, hook through, and close off. Glue the nose off-center and to the right slightly, just ⅛ in (3 mm) above the mouth.

4 TOOTH: Using yellow craft foam, cut out a single snaggletooth (and say it five times fast), about ¼ x ½ in (6 x 13 mm). Glue to the top left side of the mouth, directly below the left eye.

5 TONGUE: Using red craft foam, cut out a 1½ in (4 cm) long by ¾ in (2 cm) wide tongue shape (see pattern). Cut the flat end at a slight angle. Glue to the folded back of the mouth, so that it pokes slightly out of the right side.

6 *HAIR:* From the green fur, cut out a ¼ in (6 mm) wide and 4 in (10 cm) long strip. Glue it centered about 1¼ in (3 cm) back from the mouth. Spike liberally with your favorite non-toxic hair gel.

7 Prepare for either a fight or a Peter Jackson movie marathon surrounded by cats. Your choice.

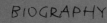

BIOGRAPHY

salbert Glugenstein is the leader of the elite superhero team, The Lava Men. He also enjoys watching cooking contests on TV, though he's a lousy chef himself. No matter what, don't try his anchovy artichoke dip. salbert gained magical powers after diving deeper into the ocean than any puppet before him and battling the ancient Giant squid of the Furthest Deep. They fought for so long that salbert actually became part squid, and the squid part salbert.

salbert the scuba Diver

LESSON 25

salbert is made using a variation on the "glasses-building" technique, as with Harold speculex (see p.32). He's mostly mask—he's made to look like most of his "wet-suit" is all sock! Just remember, if you put him in real water, he'll get all soggy. As ever, experiment with different color schemes to create alternative scuba diving super-heroes! Orange and green would look awesome! He's got a cool Lava Men song by uncle Monsterface, too.

SUPPLIES:

Templates on page 124
Red cotton sock
Cardboard
Black sticky felt
Squares of purple, yellow,
   and white craft foam
Black marker
Head fluff

1 If you want to use templates, copy the ones on page 124, then prep the red sock utilizing the "cardboard mouth" technique (see pp.17–18). I recommend a MEDIUM oval. Once the sock is reversed, add the oval of black sticky felt, cut slightly smaller than the cardboard oval, and put a small amount of head fluff in the top for structure.

2 SCUBA MASK/EYES: The eyes and mask are one mighty piece (see pattern). Using the purple craft foam, cut out a medium rectangle about 3 in (7.5 cm) long and 1½ in (4 cm) tall. Poke a hole inside the pattern and scissor out the inside to create the thin purple mask shape. Use your black marker to edge around the exterior and interior of the mask. Use the black marker to add four "rivet" dots on each corner.

3 On a clean scrap of white foam, cut out the same shape, and then shave off ⅛ in (3 mm) all the way around. Here, you're creating the interior "eyes" of the mask, so the idea is that the white foam is slightly smaller than the scuba mask, but not smaller than the hole inside it. Attach the white foam to the purple mask, again leaving no gaps in the hole and no white showing outside of the mask, so that it looks like one unbroken piece.

sss

4 Glue the mask just above the mouth. Use your marker to add dots for eyes! Which way will he look?!

5 SNORKEL: An underwater superhero has gotta breathe! Some say that the Scuba Diver can't go too deep with just a snorkel, but this snorkel is MAGIC! Using purple craft foam, cut out a 3 in (7.5 cm) long "J" shape. Using a little yellow craft foam, cut out two ½ in (13 mm) long and ¼ in (6 mm) wide rectangles. Using the black marker, edge around the yellow rectangles and the J-shape. Add three short horizontal "wrinkly" lines to the "J." Glue one of the yellow rectangles to the top of the "J," the other to the bottom of the "J." Glue the snorkel to the lower right of the mouth, letting a little bit go inside. So he can breathe!

6 Go explore the ocean together! Dive deep!

Franklin J Lopingface was long thought to be a myth. Nanaface would whisper before bed, "Close your cupboards and tuck in tight, or the Lopingface will find your little toes and bite." After an outbreak of badly bitten toes, a hunting party tracked Lopingface to Dino-skeleton Island. Lopingface was apologetic for his foot-based transgressions. Moreover, he was charming and a great host, providing everybody with a delicious lunch and excellent gift baskets.

Franklin J. Lopingface

LESSON 26

This is a playful and wacky riff on the "Face" family of designs, here taking wild liberties with the puppet's antlers. You're strongly encouraged to have some fun here, cutting a wacky shape into your own antlers. It's very likely that they will wobble about. That's for the best.

SUPPLIES:

Templates on page 124
Red/green/white striped terrycloth sock
Cardboard
Black sticky felt
Squares of yellow, orange, and pink craft foam
Black marker
Head fluff

1 If you want to use templates, copy the ones on page 124, then prep the sock utilizing the "cardboard mouth" technique (see pp.17–18). I recommend a SMALL oval. Once the sock is reversed, add the oval of black sticky felt for the mouth interior, cut slightly smaller than the cardboard oval, and put a large amount of head fluff in the top for structure.

2 EYES: Using orange craft foam, cut out two slightly mismatched rectangles, about ½ in (13 mm) x ¾ in (2 cm). Using your black marker, add pupil dots slightly off-center, both pointing inward. Glue the eyes ⅛ in (3 mm) above the mouth and ½ in (13 mm) apart.

3 TEETH: Using yellow craft foam, cut out two front buckteeth, about ¾ x ½ in (2 cm x 13 mm), and two smaller back teeth, about ½ x ½ in (13 x 13 mm). Glue the teeth to the top of the mouth, about ¼ in (6 mm) apart, making sure that the larger rectangles are the front teeth—because it's funnier that way.

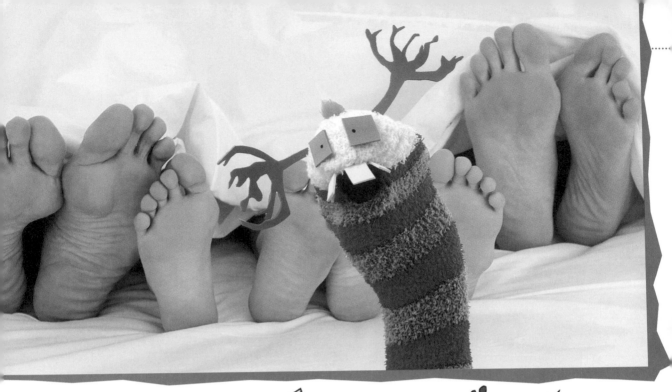

4 *HAIR:* Using the green fur, cut out a strip 1½ in (4 cm) long and about ½ in (13 mm) wide. Glue the strip of fur to the head, centered about ½ in (13 mm) behind the eyes.

5 *ANTLERS:* Using pink craft foam, cut out two 3 x 4 in (7.5 x 10 cm) rectangles. Shape the antlers based on the pattern, or create your own wacky, root-like formation. Glue the antlers directly behind the outermost point of the eyes, 1 in (2.5 cm) back, about 2 in (5 cm) apart, with green hair centered between them. Glue liberally and hold for a little extra time, and be prepared for significant wobble.

6 Cover your toes and get ready for a fancy gift basket.

Franklin J. Lopingface 85

Mozzarella is a traveler from an unknown realm of the Seven Layers of Space, with a macaroni-like head and a bike for a body. And he only speaks in pictures. But while never uttering a syllable, he has been a quiet companion to many noteworthy figures, including Stephen Hawking, Stephen King, and Nikola Tesla, to name a few. Last seen operating his legendary falafel stand on the roof of The Magician Detective's house, Mozzarella has since vanished.

Mozzarella Botticelli

LESSON 27

Like Professor Hero before him, Mozzarella is a really weird design (among a sea of weird) from The Seven Layers of Space trilogy. He's also another great example of bringing a quirky sketch to life. I long-debated whether or not to give him a real bike wheel, but thought it impractical. I have a particular fondness for his unique eye-shape, a great demonstration of how most shapes, when given a pupil, become eyes.

SUPPLIES:

Templates on page 125
Blue sock (inside out)
Cardboard
Blue sticky felt
Squares of yellow, orange, white, and black craft foam
Black and purple markers
Head fluff

1 If you want to use templates, copy the ones on page 125, then prep the sock utilizing the "cardboard mouth" technique (see pp.17–18). I recommend a MEDIUM oval. Once the sock is reversed, add the oval of blue sticky felt for the mouth interior, cut slightly smaller than the cardboard oval, and put a medium amount of head fluff in the top for structure.

2 EYES: Using yellow craft foam, cut out two 2½ x 1½ in (6 x 4 cm) rectangles. Following the pattern (or your heart), form them into eye shapes. Using the purple marker, add a dot to each eye to create the pupils. Glue the eyes ¼ in (6 mm) above the mouth and ½ in (13 mm) apart, gluing only slightly at the bottom so that they stand up.

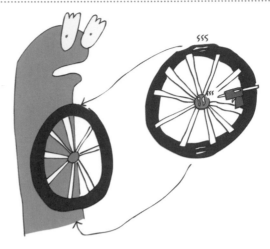

3 *WHEEL:* Using black craft foam, cut out a 4 in (10 cm) wide hollowed circle, to become the bike tube. The tube itself should end up about ½ in (13 mm) wide (see pattern). Using orange craft foam, cut out a ¾ in (2 cm) circle for the bike hub. Use black marker to edge and edge-in the circle. Using white craft foam, cut out 12 thin strips, about 1½ in (4 cm) each, as spokes. Glue them to the edge of the hub, tucked under the wheel rim, cutting off any excess that shows. Glue the wheel's hub and top to Mozzarella's body just below the mouth, centered.

4 Pack a backpack and get ready to join the search for Mozzarella Botticelli. I'm telling you, you're missing out on the falafel he sells from his stand.

Capt. Strongbear is infantry expert for the New Champions of Tomorrow, an ancient order of protectors from Sock Puppet City. Each of the three champions derives special abilities from the sacred "Masks of Blue Power." Strongbear has the power of ten strong bears, a guy named Ted, and a baby elephant that talks to the stars. His childlike mentality masks a keen tactical mind with an encyclopedic military knowledge. When he isn't training, he relaxes by watching 1980s cartoons.

Captain Strongbear

Strongbear is a pretty special puppet, stretching beyond the limits of fellow superhero puppet Salbert (see p.82), as he is essentially a carefully placed mask (and a tuft of hair and a cape). When you build the mask, several elements combine into the face, in a way bringing together lessons from glasses-building and nose placement, but making them uniform using the singular color and piece. Neat!

SUPPLIES:

Templates on page 124
Yellow sock
Cardboard
Black sticky felt
Squares of white and blue craft foam
Tuft of green fur
Square of magenta felt
Silvery rope or cord
Black and blue markers
Head fluff

1 If you want to use templates, copy the ones on page 124, then prep the sock utilizing the "cardboard mouth" technique (see pp.17–18). I recommend a LARGE oval. Once the sock is reversed, add the oval of black sticky felt for the mouth interior, cut slightly smaller than the cardboard oval, and put a large amount of head fluff in the top for structure.

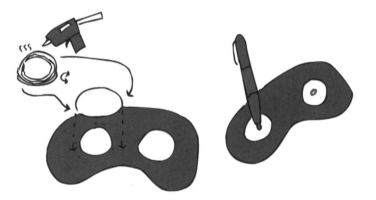

2 MASK OF BLUE POWER: The mask is the bulk of this puppet. First make the main mask shape from blue craft foam, following the pattern shown, roughly 3 in (7.5 cm) long with ¾ in (2 cm) eyeholes. Use the black marker to edge exterior perimeter and interior holes, and follow that up with edge-in around the full perimeter and eyeholes. Cut out two circles of white craft foam, each the tiniest bit bigger than the ¾ in (2 cm) eyeholes—test them out before placing them finally. Using the blue marker, draw a pupil in the center of each. Add a tiny bit of glue to the exterior of each eye and put them in place behind the hole, leaving no gaps.

3 MASK EARS: Using more of the same blue craft foam, cut out two 1 in (2.5 cm) tall and ¾ in (2 cm) wide half-ovals, edged around the perimeter and edged-in. Attach each one just behind the eyeholes.

4 MASK NOSE: Using more of the same blue craft foam, cut out a tapered 1½ in (4 cm) long, ¾ in (2 cm) wide triangle. Edge the sides and edge in. Glue this to the rest of mask so that the top nearly reaches the top of the mask and the bottom hangs over the mask bottom (see picture).

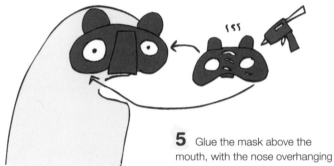

5 Glue the mask above the mouth, with the nose overhanging the mouth very slightly.

6 HAIR: Add a tiny tuft of green fur sticking up, about ½ in (13 mm) wide and 2 in (5 cm) tall, centered and about 1 in (2.5 cm) behind the mask.

7 REMOVABLE CAPE: Using pink felt, cut out a 1½ x 4 in (4 x 10 cm) rectangle. Size the silvery cord to fit around your puppeteer's wrist (generally about 6–7 in/ 15–17.5 cm) and glue either end to the top corners of the rectangle. Slip over Strongbear's head once he has been put on and is ready for deployment.

8 So long as there are no immediate threats to the universe, grab a VHS tape of some Thundercats and get ready to get vegetative with your new superhero friend.

"Sock Puppet Manor" star Tony has a knack for chasing people and hitting them on the head, making him an excellent thug. Some wonder whether Tony is "playing dumb," but it's not an act, he's just an idiot. An idiot who loves to bowl. Off-screen, Tony was Chancellor to the King of Egypt and Maker of Vases in Chief. Though not a pharaoh, he was "getting there." After his tomb was disturbed in 1932, he quickly adapted to life as a Hollywood mummy.

Tony Imhotep, Mummy

LESSON 29

Tony is a pretty experimental puppet, and the fabric takes some playing around with to get right—it's hard to give precise ideas about just how to set it. He relies largely on simply wrapping the puppet, mummy-style, but this can be an inexact science...

SUPPLIES:

Templates on page 125
Light purple sock
Cardboard
Black sticky felt
Square of white craft foam
Small piece of orange fur
Large piece of yellow felt
   (at least 40 in/100 cm)
Head fluff

1 If you want to use templates, copy the ones on page 123, then prep the sock utilizing the "cardboard mouth" technique (see pp.17–18). I recommend a LARGE oval. Once the sock is reversed, add the oval of black sticky felt for the mouth interior, cut slightly smaller than the cardboard oval, and put a medium amount of head fluff in the top for structure. Note: We'll build Tony's major features before wrapping his ancient self up last.

2 EYE: Only one eye is visible; the other is covered by his wrappings, though we don't actually ever build it. Using white craft foam, cut out one small ½ in (13 mm) eye. Using black marker, add a dot in the middle. Glue the eye ½ in (13 mm) up from the mouth, on the left side of his head.

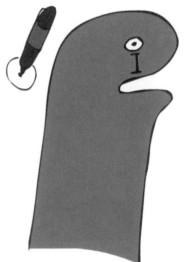

3 *TEETH:* Using white craft foam, cut out five half-oval teeth, each about ¼ in (6 mm) tall. Glue to the top of the mouth with ¼ in (6 mm) spaces between each one.

4 *HAIR:* Using orange craft fur, cut out a small tuft of orange fur, about 1 in (2.5 cm) square. Glue it centered on the head, about ¾ in (2cm) behind the eye.

5 *WRAPPING:* This is the critical detail, and it just takes some experimenting. I recommend doing the wrap over the hand of the would-be puppeteer, with the puppet on, and doing so loosely, so that you can get your hand in and out. The length varies because of different hand sizes.

Cut out one long strip of yellow felt, 1 in (2.5 cm) wide. Wrap it around the head and body, putting dabs of glue on key spots (back of head, front of head, three dabs at the front of the body, three or four on the back). Make sure at the head you wrap to cover the missing eye. In the end, all the wrapping goes about 4 in (10 cm) down the body. It doesn't all have to come from one long piece—you can supplement it if you need to. But each time you do a new piece, I recommend that you keep them "connected," so it looks like one long piece.

6 Go bowling.

Ed is a shark. Surprisingly, initially he's approachable and friendly, particularly if he isn't hungry. He's nice to hang out with, great to grab a drink or a swim with (just make sure he's eaten), but Ed can't dig deep enough inside to let anyone in. Years of attacking vulnerable swimmers have left him incapable of real friendship, always afraid that in a weak moment he might eat his new friends. Mostly because that's what he does all the time.

Ed the Emotionless Shark

LESSON 30

Ed is a pretty straightforward puppet, a sort of riff on the dinosaur theme. Lots of little teeth, big eyes on either side of the head, and some fins are a sure-fire recipe for a shark that's hard to love.

SUPPLIES:

Templates on page 124
Blue sock
Cardboard
Blue sticky felt
Squares of white and black craft foam
Three squares of blue craft foam
Head fluff
White paint

1 If you want to use templates, copy the ones on page 124, then prep the sock utilizing the "cardboard mouth" technique (see pp.17–18). I recommend a LARGE oval. Once the sock is reversed, add the oval of blue sticky felt for the mouth interior, cut slightly smaller than the cardboard oval, and put a large amount of head fluff in the top for structure.

2 EYES: Ed's eyes are unusual, mostly because he's a shark. They're far apart, and they start out black. Using black craft foam, cut out two circles, about 1 in (2.5 cm) wide each. Using white paint, add a dot to each. Glue the eyes to either side of the head in a fish-like fashion, about 2 in (5 cm) apart, with the white dot facing forward.

3 *TEETH:* Using white craft foam, cut out ten (or so) triangles measuring ½ in (13 mm) on each side. Glue them to the top rim of the mouth, spaced closely together. He's a shark, after all, and he likes to eat…

4 *FINS:* For the main dorsal fin, cut out a triangular piece about 3 in (7.5 cm) wide at the base and 2½ in (6 cm) tall from the blue craft foam (see pattern). Attach with a solid strip of glue along the bottom edge, about 2½ in (6 cm) from the mouth and centered, standing up.

5 For the side fins, using the same blue craft foam, cut out two triangular pieces 3½ in (9 cm) long and 2 in (5 cm) wide at the base (see pattern). Attach on either side of the body, about 2 in (5 cm) below the mouth.

6 Now enjoy a day together— just don't get too attached.

As seen in the soap opera "Sock Puppet Manor," Lillith Lollybottom is the boozy mom who talks to ghosts, and whose capacity to judge is only outweighed by her capacity to yell, and for her unconditional love of her family. Whom she judges all the time. Off-screen, Lillith is played by screen legend Anna Lee Shmenkman, star of the long-running soap "Your Ugly Children" and the critically acclaimed comedic spin-off "Your Ugly Children Are Jerks."

Lillith Lollybottom

LESSON 31 Lillith is an elaborate puppet whose most notable feature is her hair—utilizing a fabulous pink boa. If you can't find a boa, other fabulous pink things could be used as substitutes. The rest of her is complicated and detailed, too. She's not just a complex build physically, but emotionally, too. Alas, young girls will still want to make her.

SUPPLIES:

Templates on page 124
Light pink sock
Cardboard
Black sticky felt
Squares of pink, white, purple, and red craft foam
Hot pink boa
Optional costume necklace
Black and green markers and a pink water-based marker
Red pen
Head fluff

1 If you want to use templates, copy the ones on page 124, then prep the sock utilizing the "cardboard mouth" technique (see pp.17–18). I recommend a LARGE oval. Once the sock is reversed, add the oval of black sticky felt for the mouth interior, cut slightly smaller than the cardboard oval, and put a large amount of head fluff in the top for structure.

2 EYES: Lillith is tired and distressed, and her eyes show it. Using white craft foam, cut out two 1 in (2.5 cm) ovals. Add a black center with your trusty marker, leaving a small pupil of white. For more details, circle that black with green, and circle again with a thin black line, adding small concentric lines between the two for more pupil detail. On the exterior of the white circle of the eye, using a red pen or thin marker, add tiny red branching lines to create the sense of bloodshot eyes.

3 Using purple craft foam, cut out two eyelids about ¾ in (2 cm) deep. Edge around the top of the half-circles and in a bit, but DON'T edge the flat side of the lid. Glue the eyelid, covering about half the pupil.

4 Using pink craft foam, cut out six small thin eyelashes, each about ½ in (13 mm) long. Glue to the top of each lid. Attach the eyes 1 in (2.5 cm) above the mouth, ½ in (13 mm) apart.

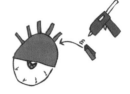

5 NOSE: Using red craft foam, cut out a tiny tapered triangle, ½ in (13 mm) long and ¼ in (6 mm) wide at the base. Edge the perimeter and in a bit. Glue ½ in (13 mm) above the mouth, between the eyes, leaving room for the lips.

6 LIPS: Using some scraps of red craft foam, cut out two tiny half-oval lip shapes about 1 in (2.5 cm) long and ½ in (13 mm) tall (see pattern). Glue above and below the mouth.

7 HAIR: Try to find something like 18 in (46 cm) of hot pink boa. Wrap it on itself, so that there are three overlapping rows that don't indicate any separation between them. Glue them down.

8 MAKE-UP: This takes some finesse, and you might want to practice on some scraps first. Find a water-based hot pink marker. On Lillith's cheeks, apply several dots and quickly "smear" them with water, creating the effect of some heavy-handed make-up use.

9 JEWELRY: Is optional, attached at the back and left loose enough for the puppeteer to get their wrist into the puppet. Pictured here, Lillith has some lovely costume jewelry. Pearls or other gaudy fake gems would work equally well.

10 Get ready for a saucy night of yelling and talking with ghosts—Lillith takes nothing from no one, but gives a whole lot back.

3 NOSE: Cut out a "Bill Murray nose shape" (see pattern) from a 1¼ x 1¼ in (3 x 3 cm) square of blue craft foam.

4 HAIR & BEARD: We'll use what you've been typically been using as "head fluff," craft batting material, for Bill Murray's beard. It works great for older gentlemen. When using the head fluff as hair, you want to build the parts—forming major sections and gluing in layers, using glue pretty liberally, as the material is soft. First form the balding widow's peak and glue down.

5 Now form two small strips for the moustache that attaches to the beard. Then form the bottom of the beard, and glue. Create two more attaching sideburns. The effect should be that of a uniform hair and beard, all attached. If you need to "patch it up" with some little areas, go for it. In Zissou's case, I also gave him a little haircut after everything was glued, trimming excess and shaping the beard.

6 RED HAT: For the patented red hat, cut out a 3 in (7.5 cm) circle of red felt, make a snip into the center of the circle with scissors, and fold the circle in on itself. Glue the seam, which will be on the back. Use more red felt and cut out one long thin strip to wrap around the bottom, mimicking the turned-up side of a wool hat. Glue the strip along the circumference of the bottom. Use the black marker to add vertical stripes along the bottom piece, creating a sense of the fabric's "piping." Glue the hat to his head, slightly to the left, allowing for a good bit of the hair to show.

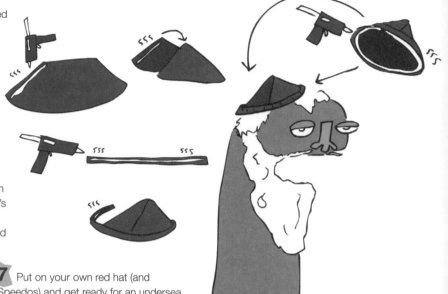

7 Put on your own red hat (and Speedos) and get ready for an undersea adventure. Maybe we can bring Salbert the Scuba Diver (see p.82), too?

Sports Robot is recreations expert for The Lava Men, iconic protectors of Dino-Skeleton Island. When not being a superhero, Sports Robot plays almost every sport: baseball, basketball, and others. Yet Sports Robot is a bit sad—all because he can't enjoy his two favorite sports: surfing and synchronized swimming. Alas, his creator fell ill just before completing Sports Robot's final component: magnificent Aqua socks. Don't be too sad, he's the best at all the other sports.

Sports Robot

LESSON 33

This is one of the craziest puppets of all... Sports Robot just might win most over-the-top sock puppet design. We've gone on and beyond the boundaries of sock-dom and built a giant robot helmet around the sock itself. Pretty impressive stuff... GO TEAM!

SUPPLIES:

Templates on page 125
Blue-toed black sock, reversed
Cardboard
Black sticky felt
Yellow felt
Square of white and light magenta craft foam, plus several squares of blue
Head fluff

1 If you want to use templates, copy the ones on page 125, then prep the sock utilizing the "cardboard mouth" technique (see pp.17–18), starting with the sock right side in so it ends reversed. I recommend a SMALL oval. Once the sock is reversed, add the oval of black sticky felt for the mouth interior, cut slightly smaller than the cardboard oval, and put a medium amount of head fluff in the top for structure.

2 EYES: Using white craft foam, cut out two squares, ½ x ½ in (13 x 13 mm). With your worn-out black marker, add a dot in the center of each. Glue them ½ in (13 mm) above the mouth and ¾ in (2 cm) apart.

3 NOSE: Using the red craft foam, cut out a ½ in (13 mm) circle. Using the black marker, edge its perimeter and interior. Glue it right between the eyes and right above the mouth.

4 INTERIOR HEADBAND: To create a weird sense of continuity, I've built the yellow headband on both his main sock head and his helmet head. Start with the sock head first: using the yellow felt, cut out a strip ⅛ in (3 mm) wide and about 7 in (17.5 cm) long. Wrap it around his head, just about ⅛ in (3 mm) above the eyes, overlapping in the back. Glue down in a few points to secure.

5 HELMET: This is complicated so needs its own sub-section! See patterns as a guide.

SHAPE: Using the blue craft foam, cut out two rectangles 2½ x 2 in (6 x 5 cm) to become the sides; one 3¼ x 2 in (8 x 5 cm) rectangle to become its back; and one 3½ x 2½ in (9 x 6 cm) rectangle to become its top. Using the inimitable black marker, add a black dot to the corner of each rectangle, mimicking "rivets." Glue at the edges, one at a time, building a half-box or helmet.

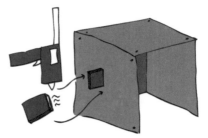

6 KNOBS: Using the red craft foam, cut out two ¾ x ¾ in (2 x 2 cm) squares. Glue each one centered and sticking out of the sides of the helmet.

7 ANTENNAS: Using the light magenta craft foam, cut out two 1 in (2.5 cm) long "rods" and two ½ in (13 mm) circles. Glue them together so that they form a one-dimensional antenna shape. Glue each antenna 1½ in (4 cm) from the front of the helmet and 1 in (2.5 cm) from the sides, facing out and standing up, or else he'll get terrible reception.

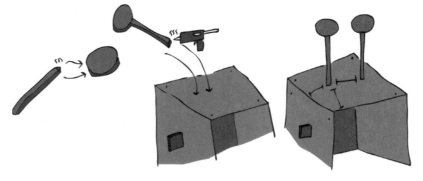

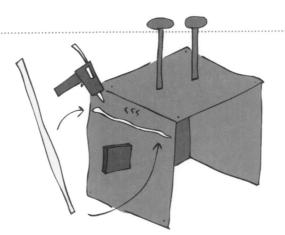

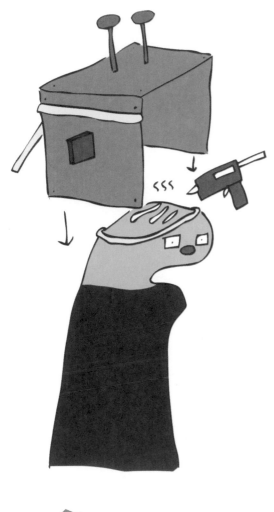

8 EXTERIOR HEADBAND:
Using the yellow felt, cut out two more strips 7 in (17.5 cm) long and ⅛ in (3 mm) wide. Glue one from the front, just below the rivets, to halfway around the back, leaving some to dangle, like cool headbands do. Repeat on the other side, overlapping when you get to the back.

9 Glue the helmet to the head with glue on top and on each side of the head. Put on your yellow headband and get ready to sweat. HIGH FIVE!

Dr. Vampire stars in "Sock Puppet Manor" and is the worst doctor ever. In general, his self-serving solution for any medical issue is to draw blood. When not being a terrible medic, Dr. Vampire is a bad vampire. Typically, he sabotages things by becoming too friendly with his victims to want to eat them. Off-screen, Dr. V is played by puppet Ben Kingsley. First bitten and turned into a vampire on the set of "Gandhi," Kingsley enjoys streaking and drinking blood.

Dr. Vampire

Dr. Vampire is a pretty fancy puppet with a lot of lightly sculpted details. His nose, teeth, and hair take a little extra time and a lighter hand, and he has the most clothing of any of the projects shown. Typically I don't do much clothing because it doesn't read that well without arms and can be a little restrictive to the puppeteer, but it felt particularly fun and funny with this over-the-top character.

SUPPLIES:

Templates on page 126
Simple gray sock
Cardboard
Two squares of black sticky felt
Squares of white, orange, purple, blue, and black craft foam
Black and red markers
Head fluff

1 If you want to use templates, copy the ones on page 126, then prep the sock utilizing the "cardboard mouth" technique (see pp.17–18). I recommend a MEDIUM oval. Once the sock is reversed, add the oval of black sticky felt, cut slightly smaller than the cardboard oval, and put a very small amount of head fluff in the top for structure.

2 EYES: For Dr. Vampire we'll be building simple lidded eyes. Using white craft foam, cut out two almond shapes, each about ¾ in (2 cm) wide and ½ in (13 mm) tall. Using your red marker, toward the center of the bottom of the almond shape, draw a small circle of red, leaving a tiny bit of white showing, for the evil vampire eyes! Outline the red circle with a thin black line.

Using purple craft foam for the eyelids, cut out two almond shapes (same size as the eyes), then cut each one a little more than in half to create a thin upper eyelid. Glue each eyelid to the top of the eye, not covering any of the pupil. Glue the eyeballs about ¾ in (2 cm) above the mouth, leaving only about ¼ in (6 mm) between them and room for the nose to fit between and below.

3 NOSE: Since Dr. Vampire is another star of soap opera "Sock Puppet Manor," he needs a fancy nose! Dr. Vampire's nose takes a bit of precision and patience. Start with a medium tapered triangle of orange craft foam, about 1 in (2.5 cm) long and ¾ in (2 cm) wide at the base. Now, using either scissors or an adult-supervised utility knife, shape the nose to match the pattern shown. Glue the nose just between the eyeballs, so that it lands right at the top of the mouth.

4 TEETH: Dr. Vampire's teeth are also lightly sculpted, using a long "denture" with vampire points (so that he can still drink blood and maintain that soap opera smile). Using white craft foam, begin by cutting out one rectangle that, when bent, will be long enough to extend across the whole upper mouth. It should start at about ½ in (13 mm) thick and 2½ in (6 cm) long. Now make small incisions at a 45-degree angle about ½ in (13 mm) from each end of one long side and cut out a strip of craft foam in between to create the "smiley fang" (see pattern). Apply glue to the other side and hold in place at the top of the mouth for at least 20 seconds.

5 HAIR: Dr. Vampire has a simple, traditional vampire's "widow's peak." Using black sticky felt, cut out a slightly oversized oval about 2 x 1½ in (5 x 4 cm). Following the pattern, create an oval with a slightly tapered front, or "peak." Stick it to the head, reinforcing with a little glue.

6 LAB COAT: The lab coat is built in four little parts and glued together, left slightly open both for flexibility and because he is "swarthy." Whenever embarking on clothing for a puppet, I'll build the pieces and try them on the puppeteered puppet before permanently gluing them. They can create movement issues and all hands are different shapes and sizes. Using white craft foam, cut out two large rectangles that are 4 x 2 in (10 x 5 cm) and two small rectangles 2½ x 1 in (6 x 2.5 cm). On one end of both of the small rectangles, trim a 45-degree angle, creating the "collar" pieces. Edge around each piece with the black marker. Glue the top collars at the top of each larger rectangle, each creating one side of the coat. Using markers, add a few details like a drawn pocket, name tag, and buttons.

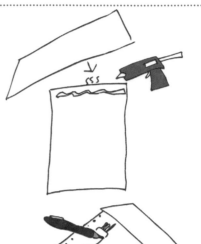

7 As Dr. Vampire is a terrible doctor (and vampire), you'll also see a lot of gross red smears on his lab coat. A light touch with some red marker and a quick bit of water to smear it can achieve this. With both sides assembled and detailed, glue each half to the body, leaving a small opening between them. Again, I recommend doing this while he is on your hand.

8 STETHOSCOPE: This is one of the more elaborate accessories among the puppet activities, but even bad doctors need stethoscopes to look official. Using black craft foam, start by cutting out a loose "t-bone" shape about 4 in (10 cm) long, and about as wide as the span of your lab coat collars (probably about 4½ in/ 11.5 cm). Next, using blue craft foam, cut out two small circles, one about half the size of the other. Edge each of these with the black marker. Glue the small blue circle on top of the larger one.

9 Glue the circles joined in the previous step to the long end of the "t-bone." To finish, glue just the tops of the stethoscope to the outer edges of the collar.

10 Engage in questionable medical diagnoses together, paying particular attention to thinking that coma patients and migraine sufferers all need blood drawn.

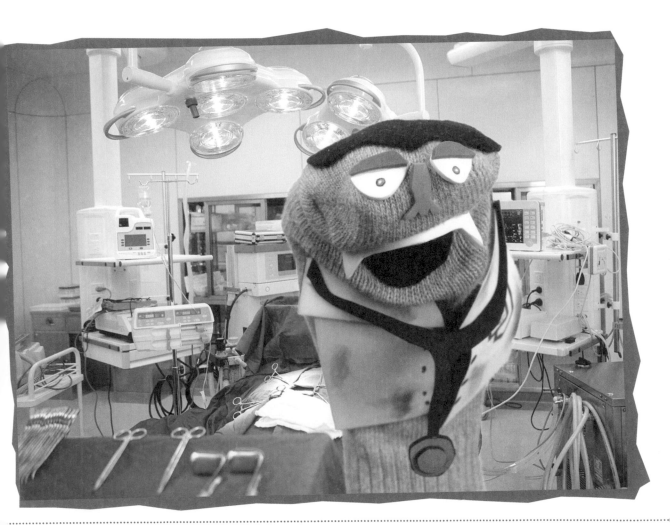

Sock puppet Amelia Earhart is much like her human counterpart—a record-setting aviator, author, and all-around Awesome Lady. The first aviatrix to pilot a solo-flight across the Atlantic, her name is also poetically super-cool ("Air Heart"). Amelia mysteriously disappeared attempting a circumnavigational flight of the globe in 1937. While many theories persist, it seems likely that aliens were involved. Or the Bermuda Triangle. Or both!

Amelia Earhart

LESSON 35

Our last "real" person is another personal hero, and a pretty tricky puppet to build. Amelia's most complicated piece is definitely her hat. Based on the real design pattern for an aviator's cap, it's broken up into several different pieces and then glued together. I've elected to do a rough gluing, per my style, but you can really finesse this one if you'd like, and the pattern would probably work with felt, too.

SUPPLIES:

Templates on page 125
Light blue sock
Cardboard
Black sticky felt
Squares of black, red, yellow, purple, pink, and brown craft foam
Yellow felt/fabric
Black marker
Head fluff

1 If you want to use templates, copy the ones on page 125, then prep the sock utilizing the "cardboard mouth" technique (see p.p.17–18). I recommend a LARGE oval. Once the sock is reversed, add the oval of black sticky felt for the mouth interior, cut slightly smaller than the cardboard oval, and put a medium amount of head fluff in the top for structure.

2 EYES: Amelia's eyes are small and fierce. Using black craft foam, cut out two ¼ in (6 mm) dots. Glue them 1 in (2.5 cm) above the mouth and 1 in (2.5 cm) apart.

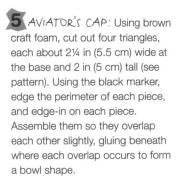

3 NOSE: Using pink craft foam, cut out a tapered triangle 1¼ in (4 cm) long and ½ in (13 mm) wide at the base. Using the ageless black marker, edge the perimeter and also edge-in. Glue the nose directly between the eyes, landing at the top of the mouth.

4 LIPS: Using red craft foam, cut out two ½ in (13 mm) semi-circles, cutting a tiny divot from the rounded side of each to create the lip shape. Glue to the top and bottom mouth pieces.

5 AVIATOR'S CAP: Using brown craft foam, cut out four triangles, each about 2¼ in (5.5 cm) wide at the base and 2 in (5 cm) tall (see pattern). Using the black marker, edge the perimeter of each piece, and edge-in on each piece. Assemble them so they overlap each other slightly, gluing beneath where each overlap occurs to form a bowl shape.

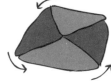

6 Cut out a single long strip 9 in (23 cm) or so (adjust as needed). Using the black marker, edge the perimeter and interior. Glue along the bottom of the cap. Still from the brown craft foam, cut out two uneven ear flaps, 1¼ in (4 cm) and 2 in (5 cm) long respectively. Using the black marker, edge the perimeters and interiors. Glue each one to the bottom edge of either side of the head (see picture). Using the black marker, add the detail "seams" and flap holes.

7 GOGGLES: From the purple craft foam, cut out goggles about 3½ in (9 cm) long (see pattern). Edge the perimeter and interior with the black marker. From the yellow craft foam, cut out two lenses, each about ¾ in (2 cm) long. Edge the perimeter with the marker. Glue the lenses to the goggles. Using the black marker, add details to the goggles such as surrounding perimeter dots for rivets, and horizontal slashes in the center. Glue the finished goggles to the cap. Glue the cap to head.

8 SCARF: Using yellow felt, cut out a strip 10 in (25 cm) long and 1 in (2.5 cm) wide. At one end, cut 1/8 in (3 mm) long and ½ in (13 mm) deep strips that remain attached to the strip, creating a scarf-like "fringe." While puppeteered, wrap the scarf and glue in place so that there is excess room for the hand to still come in and out of the puppet, and such that the "fringed" section crosses over and shows along the front.

9 Suit up and get ready for airplane adventures across the high seas. Just, um, get all of your affairs in order before leaving. Just in case!

PART

3

Extracurricular Puppet-Related Activities

We did it! Can you hear the crowd going wild? Well I can... though I pretty much always can... Friends, our journey is nearly complete, but I have a few more ideas to impart before the road comes to an end. Soon we will hold hands and high-five constantly, Sock Puppet Engineers together...

You and Your Sock Puppets

Perhaps by now you've already begun to make your own puppets and characters, complete with their own balls of idiosyncrasies, hobbies, and amusing tales, and that's awesome. Either way, I want to impart a few ideas and exercises for how to build characters and stories in this last section, and then send you on your collective and, hopefully, merry way.

For me, so much of the creation is (probably obviously by now) about the characters and the stories and worlds behind them, and I encourage you to have the same kind of fun. Like the choosing of the socks, this process goes in both directions. Sometimes the sock puppet comes first and then I discover the personality and story; sometimes I have an idea for a character and then make the sock. And sometimes it's a bit of a mix.

So let's learn more about your puppet! After you've built an original and spontaneous design, take a moment to give him/her/it a name and ridiculous back-story. In my case, I've actually given most of my Sock Puppet Portraits not only their own stories but their own social networking profiles that they maintain themselves. Some have songs, some star in soap operas—it's a wild and sprawling world, and we want you to join it.

Where does your puppet work?

What is she afraid of?

What does it like to eat?

What's his favorite book?

Where did she grow up?

TELL ME EVERYTHING! It's all in the details.

MAKE A REAL PERSON!

It's a remarkable learning experience in itself to take all that you've learned and make a sock puppet of a real person. Sock Puppet Portraits of real people are just like regular caricatures. Start with a sketch, and concentrate on a few defining details and emphasize them. A funny hat, big eyes, or proud nose can all be highlighted. Aspects of personalities can work, too. Perhaps the artist is spattered with paint? The math teacher has a little calculator? The grave digger is buried out back?

Comedy and the Comic Character

There is no reason that your sock puppet has to be funny, but there's something about them that often begs a touch of humor. As I've said about puppet history, color, and design, comedy is a subject that can and has filled much more qualified volumes. That said, I'll say a little.

I have the utmost respect for good comedy and I feel that, because of its very nature, it often doesn't get the respect that it deserves. The funny thing about funny people is that they don't like to talk about all their hard work. The less funny thing is that very often our funniest people are quite miserable (though that's a little funny, if you think about it). I believe that a complex set of evolutionary circumstances has led us to laugh at stuff, and I think this is wonderful and fascinating.

I also believe that most comedy stems from two places: a sense of surprise, and a sense of superiority. Another way of thinking of surprise is to say that we've done something to subvert our expectations. Some would argue that another source of comedy is discomfort, though I think this is a subtle sub-set of the two. Regardless, it can also be effective.

Oftentimes, these elements coincide, but they can exist exclusively. A dog driving a car is a funny surprise, but we don't feel superior to it! The classic comic character of the Very Dumb Guy does everything wrong, and in his simplest form doesn't surprise us. But he's funny because we feel superior to him! And then there's comedy in its in its purest form, the physical. Somebody falls down and we laugh. We are surprised and we also feel superior to them.

There's no real formula for building comic characters, and there are a million formulas for building comic characters.

FUN EXERCISES AND TRICKS

Give your comic character a distinct perspective: weird mailman; outer space cowboy; sad robot. Often it's modifying a well-known profession or perspective with an unexpected twist that can inspire a comic creation...
Give your comic character a flaw that has something to do with their innate goals: a weird mailman who hates paper; an outer space cowboy who is fat; a sad robot who can't go in the water.
Exaggerate them: a weird mailman hates paper so much that he destroys every phone book he sees; a fat outer space cowboy eats every taco on Mars; a sad robot who can't go in the water is built to be good at every sport, but he signs up to become a professional surfer and is destined for tragedy.
And last, if it hasn't already developed, give them a nice and redeeming element, too. Maybe that mailman always takes care of the local strays? And the cowboy is actually really brave and selfless. And the robot just wants what he can't have...
All of this stuff applies to building non-comic characters, too. I just think that everybody is funny...

Seriously, give yourself an hour every day to make a puppet. After 30 days, you'll have your own army! I did it twice! Stay committed and focused, and you'll see remarkable results. During creative droughts, I've applied this exercise to song writing and story writing, and with a little discipline the results are phenomenal. Everyone can find one extra hour a day. Go for it!

Storytelling and Narrative

If you want to do a bigger story, and you've made a puppet a day for 30 days, you've already got the cast! Narrative is defined as "a record of a passage of time." Sounds like a pretty boring story, but it could work. Storytelling has existed as a way for us to make sense of our wacky world and our over-thinking brains for longer than books, perhaps longer than speech itself. So let's try our hand at it.

Build some comic characters from the exercises above.

Now figure out who your main character is.

Give them a goal.

Now put them somewhere—that's their setting.

Put something in the way of the goal.

You've got a story!

Do they achieve their goal anyway or do they fail?

That's our conclusion!

Maybe they almost get there, fail, try harder, and then get there! That's 90 percent of Hollywood stories (and I'm not knocking it). And that last bit where you don't think they can do it, especially because of the flaw that you gave them, and then they barely do, that's very often your climax.

Once again, books and books have been written. This is a really simplified version of storytelling, but it's also fairly accurate. At its essence you have a character, a conflict, and a place where all the stuff happens. All the twists and turns and fun stuff that happen come as you tell it. The richer the character you've built, the more you know about them, the more interesting the story gets.

The best way to get good at storytelling, like puppet-building and pretty much everything ever, is to do it.

Now Put On a Show!

Though I strongly encourage original ideas, I also highly recommend staging favorite scenes from classics. "Gone with the Wind" and "Death of a Salesman" are crying out for new sock puppet interpretations! As is "Dallas" and, most importantly, "Perfect Strangers."

What's your story?

A fantastic undersea adventure?

A day in the life of a dog?

An over-the-top buddy pic with a huge budget co-starring me (I await your call)?

Really: tell your story, and show it to people. Videotape it and put it up on the internet. I wanna see what you made—find me at martystuff.com and come and share!

And don't forget to network your puppets, too! Create a gathering for yourself, other sock puppet makers, and one another's puppets—it's the ultimate social mixer and awesomely weird! Whether it's online or in person—invite me!

So Long and Farewell

Congratulations, you are now a certified Sock Puppet Engineer. I trust that you will utilize your new powers with responsibility, aplomb, and, above all else, while waving your arms around like a crazy person. I hope this was, if nothing else, enormous fun.

When I mention throughout the book that I want to see what you come up with, I hope you know that I mean it.

Find me and show me and tell me, there's nothing that would make me happier.

Thanks so much for reading, and thanks for possibly trying some of the stuff out. And, most importantly: keep on being awesome.

Templates

Here are the templates needed to complete all the projects. Don't feel you have to use them; they are mainly here as a guide. The good thing about sock puppets is that they are perfectly imperfect; so I tend to cut out most things by eye. It's quicker that way and means every sock puppet is unique. Some of the templates require you to enlarge them to twice the size. To do this, simply place the page on a photocopier and enlarge it by 200%. Or you can draw it freehand if you'd rather.

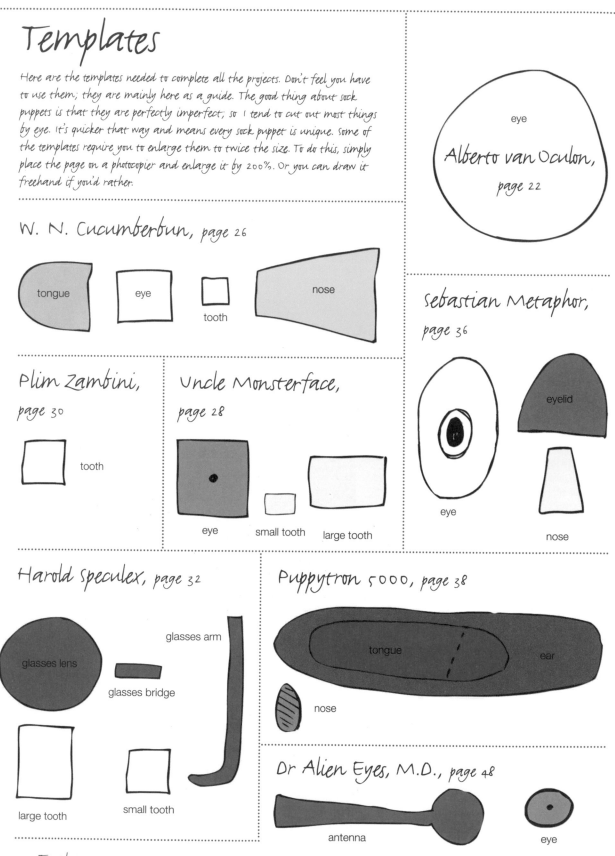

Alberto van Oculon, page 22

eye

W. N. Cucumberbun, page 26

tongue

eye

tooth

nose

Plim Zambini, page 30

tooth

Uncle Monsterface, page 28

eye

small tooth

large tooth

sebastian Metaphor, page 36

eyelid

eye

nose

Harold Speculex, page 32

glasses lens

glasses arm

glasses bridge

large tooth

small tooth

Puppytron 5000, page 38

tongue

ear

nose

Dr Alien Eyes, M.D., page 48

antenna

eye

Penelope Durtlinger, *page 40*

eye

eyelid

lips

eye patch

nose

The Nutty Bunny, *page 44*

nose

teeth

big eye

small eye

inner and outer ears

Cousin Wizardface, *page 46*

hat

tooth

star

ear

eye

Baron Cladius von Cudgel, *page 50*

nose

moustache

eyelid

nose

tooth

eye

lips

Lady MacBreath, *page 52*

hair

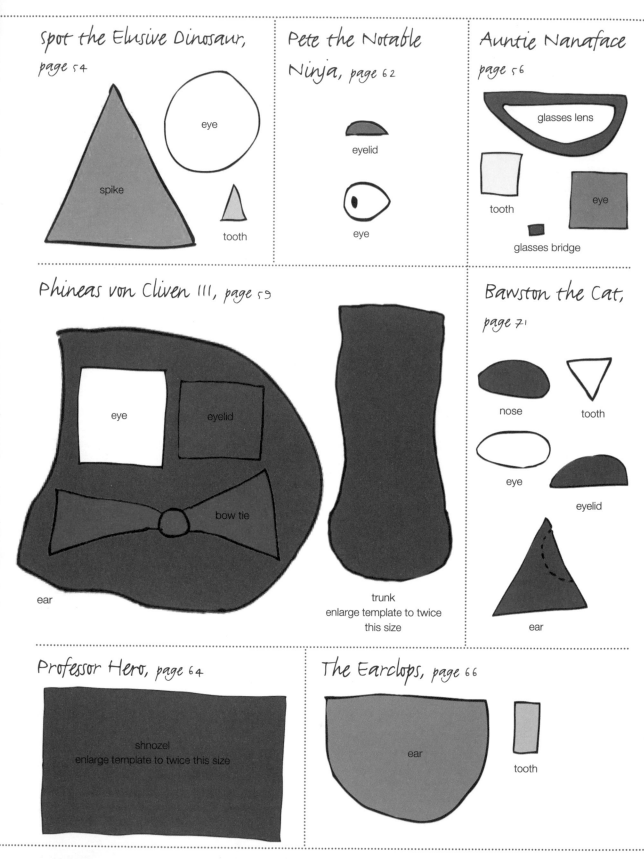

Spot the Elusive Dinosaur, page 54

eye

spike

tooth

Pete the Notable Ninja, page 62

eyelid

eye

Auntie Nanaface, page 56

glasses lens

tooth

eye

glasses bridge

Phineas von Cliven III, page 59

eye

eyelid

bow tie

ear

trunk
enlarge template to twice
this size

Bawston the Cat, page 71

nose

tooth

eye

eyelid

ear

Professor Hero, page 64

shnozel
enlarge template to twice this size

The Earclops, page 66

ear

tooth

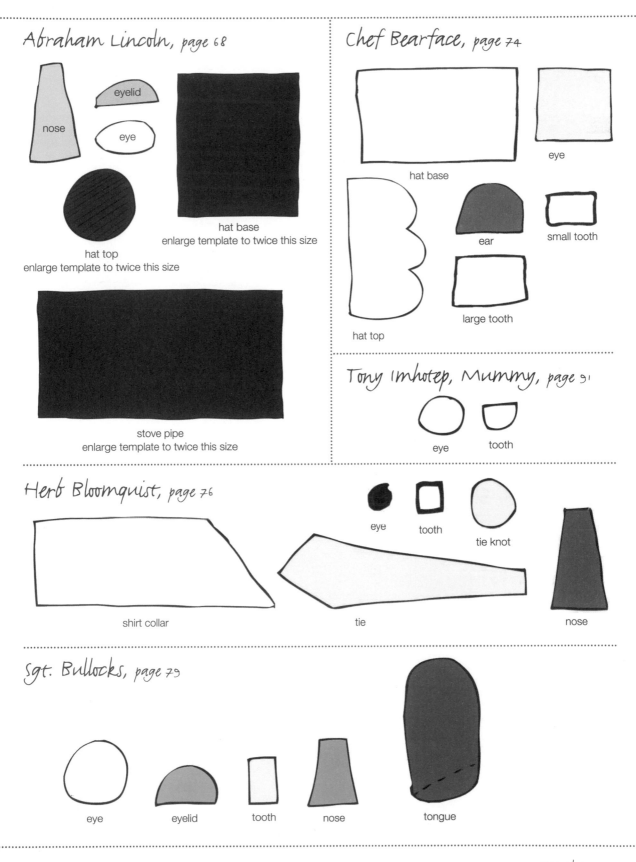

Abraham Lincoln, *page 68*

nose

eyelid

eye

hat top
enlarge template to twice this size

hat base
enlarge template to twice this size

stove pipe
enlarge template to twice this size

Chef Bearface, *page 74*

hat base

eye

ear

small tooth

large tooth

hat top

Tony Imhotep, Mummy, *page 91*

eye

tooth

Herb Bloomquist, *page 76*

shirt collar

tie

nose

eye

tooth

tie knot

Sgt. Bullocks, *page 79*

eye

eyelid

tooth

nose

tongue

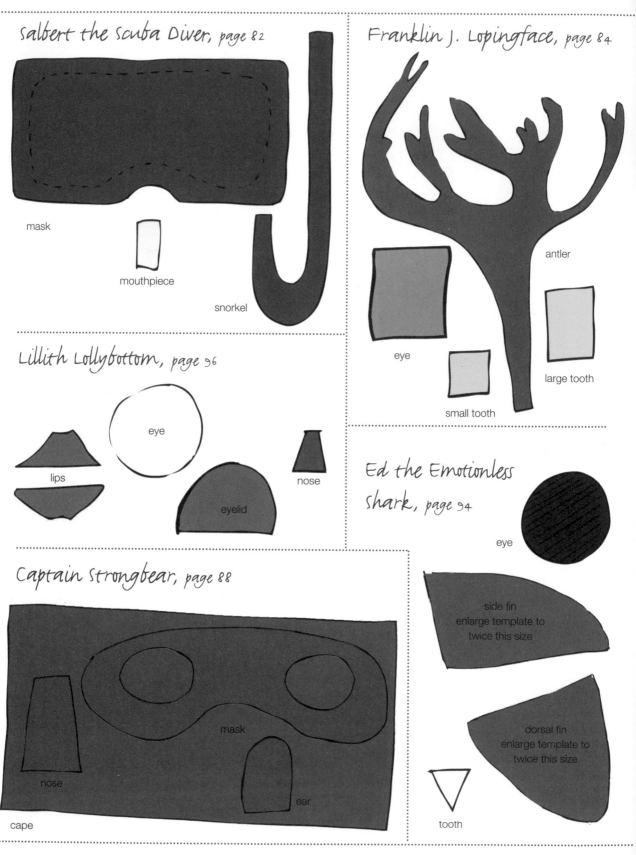

Salbert the Scuba Diver, *page 82*

mask

mouthpiece

snorkel

Franklin J. Lopingface, *page 84*

antler

eye

large tooth

small tooth

Lillith Lollybottom, *page 96*

eye

lips

eyelid

nose

Ed the Emotionless Shark, *page 94*

eye

side fin
enlarge template to
twice this size

dorsal fin
enlarge template to
twice this size

tooth

Captain Strongbear, *page 88*

mask

nose

ear

cape

Bill Murray/
Steve Zissou, pg

nose

eye

eyelid

hat
cut along dotted line

Mozzarella Botticelli,
page 86

wheel, spoke, and hub
enlarge templates to twice this size

Sports Robot, page 103

nose

eye

knob

antenna

small helmet piece

large helmet piece

eye

Amelia Earhart, page 110

lips

goggle eye

goggles

eye

nose

cap section

ear flap

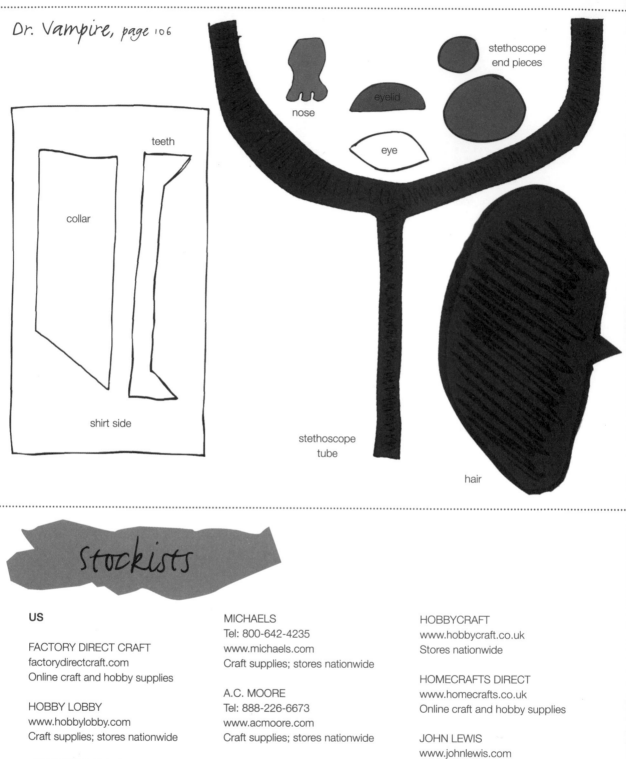

Dr. Vampire, page 106

teeth

collar

shirt side

nose

eyelid

eye

stethoscope end pieces

stethoscope tube

hair

Index

ACKNOWLEDGMENTS

The list of great creative inspirations could go on forever, but I'd be remiss not to acknowledge those who've taught me the most about storytelling and character: Edward Gorey, Theodore Geisel, Joss Whedon, Douglas Adams, JRR Tolkien, Stephen King, Joseph Campell, Wes Anderson, and Maurice Sendak.

This particular book also owes enormous spiritual debts to the How-To books of Ed Emberly, Quentin Blake, Strunk & White, and Lao Tzu, all of whom taught me more technique in a page than four years of higher education. The gifted teacher from my public education that deserves more than a sentence (and less than twelve beers) is Anthony Rizzitano. Thanks, Rizz.

And it goes (almost) without saying that this book and my work would never have happened if it weren't for the genius of Jim Henson. His boundless imagination is an inspiration to me every day. I owe everything to him, and could only ever hope to stand in his shadow.

I'd like to thank the good people at Cico Books for this opportunity. Clare, Pete, Cindy, Sandra, and the variety of inevitably clever people who've helped that I don't even know about or don't yet know as I type this. They've been nothing but supportive of my wacky vision, and words can't express my gratitude.

And I'd like to thank all of my robust family of friends. There are too many to name. I'm tremendously lucky to be in the midst of an embarrassment of intelligent and interesting people who consistently put up with and sometimes participate in my bewildering shenanigans. You're the best, you guys.

And, most importantly, I'd like to thank everybody who has supported my work, Martystuff, and the Sock Puppet Portraits, over the years. Thanks for taking away a little piece of The Ultimate Gift of Love.

AND OF COURSE I'D LIKE TO THANK YOU.

thank you